VATICAN II AND BEYOND

VATICAN II AND BEYOND

The Changing Mission and Identity of Canadian Women Religious

Rosa Bruno-Jofré,
Heidi MacDonald,
and Elizabeth M. Smyth

McGill-Queen's University Press
Montreal & Kingston • London • Chicago

ISBN 978-0-7735-5148-0 (cloth)
ISBN 978-0-7735-5149-7 (paper)
ISBN 978-0-7735-5263-0 (ePDF)
ISBN 978-0-7735-5264-7 (ePUB)

Legal deposit fourth quarter 2017
Bibliothèque nationale du Québec

Printed in Canada on acid-free paper that is 100% ancient forest free (100% post-consumer recycled), processed chlorine free

This book has been published with the help of a grant from the Canadian Federation for the Humanities and Social Sciences, through the Awards to Scholarly Publications Program, using funds provided by the Social Sciences and Humanities Research Council of Canada.

McGill-Queen's University Press acknowledges the support of the Canada Council for the Arts for our publishing program. We also acknowledge the financial support of the Government of Canada through the Canada Book Fund for our publishing activities.

Cover image:
Title: *En medio de nosotros / Between Us* (inspired by Kandinsky's work)
Artists: Gorka Eizaguirre and Mireia Lizundia Eizaguirre
School: La Salle Zarautz
Teacher: Idurre Aguirregomezcorta Arrojeria
Photography: Curator Dr Ana Jofré
Photograph from the exhibition Experiencing the Catholic Faith, Centro Carlos Santamaria, Universidad del Pais Vasco, San Sebastian
Curator: Dr Ana Jofré

Library and Archives Canada Cataloguing in Publication

Vatican II and beyond : the changing mission and identity of Canadian women religious / Rosa Bruno-Jofré, Heidi MacDonald, and Elizabeth M. Smyth.

Includes bibliographical references and index.
Issued in print and electronic formats.
ISBN 978-0-7735-5148-0 (cloth).--ISBN 978-0-7735-5149-7 (paper).--ISBN 978-0-7735-5263-0 (ePDF).--ISBN 978-0-7735-5264-7 (ePUB)

1. Catholic women--Religious life--Canada.

BX1421.3.V38 2017 282.082 C2017-904739-6
C2017-904740-X

Contents

Figures and Tables

FIGURES

TABLES

VATICAN II
AND BEYOND

INTRODUCTION

Women Religious after Vatican II: Navigating the Turbulent Waters of the "Age of Fracture"

Rosa Bruno-Jofré, Heidi MacDonald, and Elizabeth M. Smyth

The year 2015 marked the fiftieth anniversary of the closure of the Second Vatican Council (Vatican II). The council, which broadly aimed at aligning the Church with the modern world, is considered the most significant event in the history of contemporary Roman Catholicism. The impact of the council on women religious, who engaged with the reforms with unprecedented enthusiasm, far exceeded the changes expected by the hierarchy of the Church. The decline of religious life is often blamed on the Second Vatican Council, but this book documents and demonstrates the greater complexity of the issues involved.

The reforms of Vatican II were set against the backdrop of a world that moved through the upheavals of the "long 1960s"[1] into the "age of fracture,"[2] in which unstable configurations translated into a social imaginary where contingency and choice were the dominant values. The period after the long 1960s was also a time of transition to the new political setting of the 1990s post-Cold War era. The post-Cold War era dragged into the present residual elements from both colonial times and the Cold War, in the forms of regionalism, ethnic exclusivism, and so on, tainting parts of Europe, and Africa. To an important extent, the history of Rwanda, relevant here for chapter 2, reveals the limits of exporting ideologies and belief systems – in this case Christian, with a heavy Catholic presence.

The fifty years subsequent to the Second Vatican Council were the setting of an intense historical journey that brought both dramatic changes – to ways of being, seeing others, and human rights – and escalating conflicts. In those fifty years, intense religious feelings coexisted with intense processes of secularization.[3] The age of fracture, clearly represented by the cultural struggles of the 1980s, is considered a time of disaggregation; it gave room to multiple possibilities of the self and multiple changes in perception and world outlook.[4] Plurality acquired a new meaning for women religious, since they could no longer position themselves as purveyors of absolute truth.[5]

The authors contributing to this collection address the central question of how Canadian women religious envisioned and lived out the changes in religious life, their own congregations, the Church, and society at large, as well as their insertion in turbulent worlds. They do so in various ways: through an analysis of a national organization (the Canadian Religious Conference), through the experience of a congregational leader, and through the experience of rank-and-file sisters. Of necessity, a related question emerged: How were identities reconstructed and roles redefined?

The chapters in this book explore the questions of how women religious experienced the internal and external changes of the long 1960s and beyond in a destabilizing environment, and how they worked out the resignification of their vision and mission at the personal and collective level. Congregations had to deal with a historical misalignment between the regulated life of their congregations and the world. Such misalignment was already evident in the 1950s when there were early attempts to move in new directions.

The book opens with "Smaller Numbers, Stronger Voices: Women Religious Reposition Themselves through the Canadian Religious Conference, 1960s–80s." Heidi MacDonald analyzes the Canadian Religious Conference (CRC) and the ways in which women and men religious used this collective outlet to work out a more equitable relationship with the ecclesiastical authorities by undertaking and conveying authoritative systematic studies about their own situation in relation to the context. CRC's participation in major developments, such as their submission to the Royal Commission on the Status of Women in 1966, shows that the leaders of congregations were in tune with the movements of the time. (Nonetheless, congregations could have various levels of openness, awareness, and desire for change, as shown in chapter 2.) Of those, the commitment to social justice emerged powerful in Catholic discourse, acquiring its own connotations.

The chapter by MacDonald, the first study of its kind, provides the necessary framework to understand the unique experiences related in the other two chapters – "The Missionary Oblate Sisters: Renewal and the Tortuous Journey of the Prophetic Feminist Vision of Alice Trudeau," by Rosa Bruno-Jofré, and "Living Religious Life on a Broad Canvas: Vatican II and Sister Mary Alban (Bernadette) Bouchard, CSJ," by Elizabeth Smyth. These chapters go deep into the experience of particular sisters and situations in order to engage the reader in the layers of intentionality and meanings that emerged during the process of change. They examine historically situated processes of rebuilding individual and collective identities that took place at the intersection of late modernity with the social and political waves of the second part of the twentieth century that would then shift toward the post-Cold War era. The dominant tool employed by Smyth is biography. Bruno-Jofré relies on contextualization of various points in time and eclectic articulations of Pierre Bourdieu's notion of "field," Quentin Skinner's theory of meaning and intentionality, and the concept of "social imaginary" derived from Charles Taylor. She also uses feminist theories in her analysis of the gendered politics of the institutions. While Smyth works with a pontifical congregation rooted in seventeenth-century France, Bruno-Jofré deals with a diocesan congregation founded at the beginning of the twentieth century in the large diocese of Saint-Boniface, in a rather recently created Canadian province, Manitoba. Both chapters take a *longue durée* approach.

The three chapters are distinct. However, dominant themes in current historical research on congregations of women religious span all three: demographic changes; feminism; the professionalization of religious life; drastic changes in governance; paradigmatic changes in theological epistemologies; a reformulated commitment to social justice; the struggle with loss, pain, and grief; the reframing of Aboriginal issues; and the intersection of globalism and localism.

Perhaps the greatest evidence of fracture in congregations of women religious in the immediate post-Vatican II era is the withdrawal of a significant number of sisters from their congregations. The number of sisters in Canada fell from approximately 66,000 to 44,127 between 1965 and 1975.[6] While the number of withdrawals peaked in 1972 at more than eight hundred, and then levelled off by the mid-1970s, the related drop in entrants, which also began at the time of Vatican II, never reversed.[7] In fact, dozens of congregations of women religious in Canada have not received an entrant in the last fifty years. There is, therefore, a second major demographic change at work in congregations in the post-Vatican II era: aging. Whereas more than half of all women religious in Canada were under 55 at the time of the Second Vatican Council, the subsequent dearth of entrants meant that only 3 percent of women religious were under 55 at the turn of the century, and that the total number of women religious had dropped to 20,089.[8]

These stark demographic changes have impacted congregations of women religious deeply, particularly in their human resource capacity. In the post-Vatican II era, few congregations were able to commit to the institutional staffing of schools and hospitals as they had in the past. However, the high expectations placed on women religious in these traditional lines of work did not continue either. The demographic changes, which some argue began as early as 1941,[9] intersected with provincial governments' increased responsibility for social services, which in some provinces – most notably Quebec – pushed sisters out of their traditional work. A third line intersecting with decreasing human resource capacity was the Decree on the Adaptation and Renewal of the Religious Life (*Perfectae Caritatis*, 1965), which encouraged religious congregations to reconsider the charism of their founder and work more directly with the poor. Most congregations interpreted *Perfectae Caritatis* as a call to reorient themselves away from work in large institutions in favour of smaller scale social endeavours, with various, often unexpected, political shades, including work in Latin America and Africa. Many of these new commitments responded to the political positioning of the Holy See. Although demographic changes confirm that congregations of women religious were experiencing internal fracture in the decade after Vatican II, and the number of sister-teachers fell by almost three-quarters and sister-nurses by approximately half, it cannot be suggested that demographic changes, and especially the reduced human resource capacity, *caused* the fracture. The fracture was as multifaceted as was secular society and caused by intersecting influences, including changing goals of the broader Church and state.

Still, it is difficult to separate the issues of reform as expressed in *Perfectae Caritatis* and the Dogmatic Constitution on the Church (*Lumen Gentium*, 1964) from the human resource crisis in congregations that became particularly stark in the late 1960s. On the one hand, the loss of one-quarter of membership across congregations in the decade after

Vatican II meant that the congregations could not fulfill their institutional obligations, let alone respond to new requests, such as Pope John XXIII's call for missions in Latin America in 1961. On the other hand, it can be argued that the return of the congregations to charism exercises, as specifically mandated in *Perfectae Caritatis*, gave room to new ministries and a focus on social justice – although in some cases that focus was enacted individually, and in others it did not go beyond acquiring a new language. All these considerations give rise to two questions: Did congregations such as the Oblate Sisters leave schools because of human resource challenges, or did they leave because of redefined priorities? How deep was their commitment to social justice, articulated in various ways in their mission statements?

All three chapters of this book engage with women religious' *feminisms*. The period under study is known for its women's movement, often described as "second-wave feminism," although the wave analogy has been widely criticized for failing to appreciate the continuity of women's campaigns for political and economic equality over centuries.[10] In fact, congregations of women religious developed idiosyncratic understandings of feminisms – not only because their large membership has never supported a single view of women's rights or roles, but also because of the unique convent environment and broader issues of governance within the patriarchal setting of the Church. As members of closed, self-governing, women-only organizations, congregations of women religious embraced some feminist principles (such as rights to higher education and job opportunities) independently of secular feminist movements.[11] In the same vein, Marta Danylewycz argued that feminism and women's right to vote in provincial elections came late to Quebec because those women who might have led it were in the convent enjoying leadership roles.[12] In such ways women religious were, in Helen Ebaugh's words, "unwitting feminists" long before the 1960s.[13] "Under-the-radar" feminists might be a more apt description, because the women themselves had to have been aware that the patriarchal church might not appreciate their identification with feminism. One cannot neglect, however, the class element in the convents that was also addressed in the process of renewal. Certainly the subjects of chapters 2 and 3, sisters Alice Trudeau and Mary Alban, exercise forms of autonomy in their communities at a point when women in society at large were leaving the "straightjacket of gender."[14]

Groundbreaking American feminist Betty Friedan named the "emergence of the American nun from the cloister to define and assert her personhood in society" as one of the most significant aspects of the 1960s women's movement.[15] No high-profile Canadian feminist ever made a similar claim; yet again, sisters Alice Trudeau and Mary Alban are examples of sisters who fulfilled their personhood after Vatican II in ways that must have been unimaginable to them before the Second Vatican Council. Moreover, the leadership of the CRC repeatedly asserted the collective personhood of women religious after Vatican II, particularly by insisting on the prophetic voice of the religious and their right to be heard by the episcopacy. Women religious' entrance into the fields of theology and canon law, as well as their participation in the Canadian Senate and the United Nations, are further examples of their leadership well beyond the convent. The literature on second-wave feminism in Canada is not yet well developed, but we hope that this book will help to ensure that women religious are included.

The majority of Canadian women religious were members of active congregations whose charism was oriented to service of God through service of neighbour, in contrast to contemplative congregations whose interaction with secular people was very limited. Thus, they worked in the fields of education, social service, and health care. As Smyth has argued, in the course of the twentieth century these fields professionalized, and the women religious who worked in congregationally owned and administered institutions needed to keep up with the times and to acquire the necessary credentials.[16] The Church and the congregations were deeply aware of the challenges that this professionalization presented. On the one hand, it was essential that sister-workers were adequately trained; on the other, sending sister-workers for further education to acquire the necessary knowledge and skills would deprive the institutions of much needed staff. There were other factors as well. In the first decades of the twentieth century and until the 1950s, there are testimonies that bishops, in line with the anti-liberal and anti-modernist tones of the Magisterium, were concerned that the sisters who attended secular institutions would be exposed to secular anti-religious ideas.[17]

The chapters in this collection document the internal challenges that such professionalization presented. Not all sisters became professional, or were given the opportunity to do so, although their situation changed after the renewal process of the late 1960s and 1970s. Smyth documents how Sister Mary Alban was plucked from her elementary school classroom and sent to be a full-time university student in order to acquire the credentials necessary to serve as a secondary school teacher in the rapidly expanding secondary school system. Sister Alice Trudeau, as recounted in Bruno-Jofré's chapter, entered the Missionary Oblate Sisters in 1953, when she was eighteen. It was a period when the sisters, under the influence of Sister Louis de France (Albina Laberge), had begun to go back to school and obtain degrees, thus being exposed to emerging ideas in education, psychology, and theology. Laberge, who had entered the congregation in 1910, was convinced from very early on that education empowered the sisters. She was faced with significant resistance to her convictions; nevertheless, under her guidance, Trudeau finished high school, completed a bachelor of arts degree, and obtained a teaching certificate. When she left teaching in 1977, she began to focus her energies on what had been her main preoccupation: her spiritual growth and ability to serve people spiritually and social-psychologically, at both the individual and the community level.[18]

One of the most dramatic changes in religious life brought about by the implementation of *Perfectae Caritatis* was the change required in congregational governance. Congregations were directed to become more collaborative in their decision-making – both with respect to overall congregational direction and at an individual level. While a vow of obedience still bound individual members to the congregation, each sister was to become engaged in a discussion of where and how she should be deployed. The three chapters in this book show how individuals and congregations responded to this change. MacDonald provides a framework to situate the work of the congregations within the larger Canadian organized network of women and men religious, both in terms of religious responses to the world and in terms of the broader historical setting. Smyth traces how Sister Mary Alban, by following her superior's instructions, resumed the writing she put aside when she entered the convent. Sister Mary Alban relied on the community's support as she undertook activities that brought her into direct opposition to civil authorities. Bruno-Jofré provides the case of Sister Alice Trudeau as an illustration of how the experience of a congregational leader could be both in harmony and at odds with the overall direction a community followed. Bruno-Jofré shows the difficulties encountered by the Oblate Sisters in building a coherent new ideology, when they moved away from a centralist authoritarian model (based on obedience and ignoring Western liberal values) and embraced a collaborative model of religious virtuosity,

As communities grew to accept individual missions and moved away from the large institutions that were not only branded with the congregational names but also staffed by women religious garbed in readily identifiable habits, community identities wavered. The work of sociologist and Sister of Charity Patricia Wittberg (2000) and historian of English congregations Carmen Mangion traces how the implementation of the reforms of Vatican II, and the subsequent exodus of members, challenged congregational identity. The subjects of the chapters by Smyth and Bruno-Jofré remained within their congregations and claimed congregational identity, but both lived and worked at geographical, theoretical, and theological distances from the majority of the members of their congregations.[19]

The intersections of ways of thinking theology with philosophical, social, and economic paradigmatic shifts, the emphasis on context to understand authorial statements, and the development of feminist paradigms that questioned epistemologies generated new tools and approaches. The decisions made by the women religious examined in this book clearly indicate that development. It is worth noting that the search for a renewed vision and mission was not just a response to secularization; it was a way of being reborn as Catholic women. It can certainly be argued that, in most cases, the process of change and the forms of engagement with the world became a way of ending a historical cycle. The ordination of women was and continues to be a contentious, unresolved issue. In MacDonald's words, "the act of the CRC complaining to the state about the Catholic Church's lack of women's ordination or 'altar girls' is revolutionary." What was at stake was clearly a matter of power. MacDonald concludes that the broad base of the membership – both male and female religious – gave the CRC executive confidence and power to make this kind of statement; however, the statement did not go far.

As Rosemary Radford Ruether has written, as a result of their engagement in Vatican II, many women religious undertook the study of theology and played an active role in the formation of feminist theology. Smyth examines how attendance at the Divine Word Centre in London, Ontario, equipped Sister Mary Alban with a conceptual framework in which to analyze her own experience as a religious. Further, as Sister Ellen Leonard has written, the opening of the traditionally male schools of theology to not only women students but also women professors gave women religious both a new perspective and a new role to play in the study and practice of theology.[20] As Smyth's chapter illustrates, eco-theology, especially the work of Thomas Berry, had a profound influence on Sister Mary Alban. The chapter by Bruno-Jofré includes an explanation of how Alice Trudeau deepened her spiritual formation before becoming the leader of her congregation by pursuing a formation in Ignatian spirituality in the 1970s that took her to the Jesuit Institute of Formation in St Louis, Missouri, for one year, followed by a one-month retreat in Manresa, Spain. According to Trudeau's own account, she had adopted the Rogerian (after Carl Rogers) approach in her Ignatian spirituality. She had then moved on to Christian meditation. Finally, following her frustrated attempt to enact a vision of change and social justice for her congregation, when she graduated from the Institut de Formation Humaine Intégrale de Montréal, she had formed for herself the goal of accompanying persons or groups in the process of actualization of human vital strengths.[21] Trudeau then pursued her evangelical vision in Africa.

As in the case of many secular reforms, the impetus for Vatican II long preceded the actual calling of the council. In the 1950s the Vatican initiated the discussion of reforms, such as changes in the habit, and generated new organizational structures for further global communications, such as the Union of International Superiors General (1951), the Canadian Religious Conference (1954), and the Conference of Major Superiors (1956) in the United States. Not only did Vatican II *not initiate* the mentioned reforms, the paradigmatic shift that the council generated also had an *incomplete* quality. The resolutions were issued within the parameters of a hierarchical patriarchal institution; the council did not address gender issues, human rights, or even the place of women in the Church. Many women religious were very hopeful about the promise of Vatican II, but few found their hopes fulfilled, as can be seen in the numbers leaving and in the expressed disappointment of some who remained. Sister Alice Trudeau was among those frustrated by the limitations of reform and by the interplay of residual and new elements in the life of the congregation. She found a new mission by breaking boundaries, while Sister Mary Alban took an activist direction on her own (albeit with support from her congregation).

The feminist perspectives developed by the sisters varied depending on their familiarity with the growing body of theological scholarship, grounded in feminism, that took various epistemological stands from the late 1960s. A maternal feminism – a form of feminism embedded on women's identity as nurturers, mothers, and caregivers – seems to be at work as the substratum. Maternal feminism was not a far reach from the complementarity thesis articulated by the Church. Some congregations quickly adopted maternal feminism. Trudeau herself used the complementarity thesis – but within a framework that demanded changes in relations of power within the Church. Mary Daly's *Church and the Second Sex*, published in 1968 and widely read in the early process of renewal, was also an important influence.

The sisters made serious attempts to re-signify their mission in light of a commitment to social justice. In practice, those attempts most commonly took the form of individual missionary endeavours, since the congregations often failed to build a common intentionality. What made the post-Vatican II involvement unique was the way the congregations interpreted the documents – influenced, to an important extent, by the reading of Vatican II in Latin America. An example of such influence was an understanding of social justice as a call to live the radicalness of the Gospel. Many sisters took this call beyond institutional limits, as illustrated in this collection. The post-conciliar commitment to social justice responded to a paradigm that differed dramatically from the Catholic social teaching that had begun with Leo XIII's *Rerum Novarum* (Of New Things) in 1891. This encyclical responded to the radicalization of workers and the political movements that developed as a response to growing inequities between rich and poor, by seeking class harmony, encouraging mixed [trade] unions (owners – even nobility – workers, and peasants), making a strong case for private property, and rejecting socialism as an economic system. In the pope's view, the socialists would destroy religion. In the encyclical, he advocated a return to some kind of medieval guild and called for the common good.[22] The encyclical generated within the Church, particularly in Europe and Latin America, currents and groups that sought to channel social action and reach out to the working class; some of these groups even questioned the mixed unions. However, their attempts often faced opposition from important sectors of the Church that were allied with conservative parties in many countries. *Quadragesimo Anno* (After Forty Years), the encyclical by Pious XI, continued the emphasis on class collaboration rather than class conflict, just salaries, and moral renewal as a prerequisite for social renewal ("a Christian reform of morals"). The encyclical also introduced the principle of subsidiarity – that central authority should not deal with matters that could be better handled at the local level.[23]

The Church's preoccupation with social justice, as communicated in the encyclicals, coexisted with national churches' alliances with dictatorships, their involvement in colonization projects, and national Catholicism in Franco's Spain (1939–1975), particularly in its early stage. The discourse on social justice entered a new phase with the Cold War and broadened to include the struggle against communism. Catholic schools offered as varied a landscape as the Church itself, from teaching congregations working with the rich and powerful, to the same but with provisions for the poor, to charity work, and finally to those working exclusively with the poor. The encyclical *Mater et Magistra* (Mother and Teacher) issued by John XXIII in 1961 addressed the social question with a language of reform, that is, a developmentalist language. The document differentiated developed from underdeveloped countries and both of these from countries on the way to development, using Harry Truman's categories of economic development. It also drew attention to inequality among individuals and nations and the need for agrarian reform.[24] The encyclical was initially influential at the point when radicalization among Catholics working in social projects in Latin America had begun, their way paved by ideas from liberation theology.

Drawing on these three encyclicals – *Rerum Novarum*, *Quadragesimo Anno*, and *Mater et Magistra*, considered key proclamations of Church teachings – the authors of the Vatican II *Gaudium et Spes* (The Joys and Hopes), the Pastoral Constitution on the Church in the Modern World (1965), challenged the Church to live the Gospel through actions that support the dignity of the individual and the common good.[25] The document aimed at interpreting contemporary conditions in light of the Gospel. In Hollenbach's words, "the document makes a major contribution to modern Catholic social teaching by presenting more explicitly developed theological grounds for the Church's social engagement than are found in the earlier social encyclicals."[26] The reception of *Gaudium et Spes* was in many cases influenced by liberation theology, which reached congregations from South to North and across the Atlantic. The Medellín document (1968), a result of the Conference of Latin American Bishops in Medellín, Colombia, would become a powerful inspiration, particularly for congregations working in complex social settings, often conflict-ridden, in Latin America and beyond.

From the late 1960s, a discourse of structural change, expressed in a language of social justice, class, and oppression, went along with alternative transformative projects, particularly in Latin America. The fear of mixing with the secular forces of change and radical ideologies was left behind.[27] However, the 1980s, and the American president of the time, Ronald Reagan, were to signal a bifurcation and an attempt on the part of the Holy See to stop this process, clearly revealed by events in Nicaragua and Brazil.

The Aboriginal peoples' denunciation of residential schools because of the abuse, suffering, and destruction of culture they inflicted, shook the congregations who had been involved. The Missionary Oblate Sisters, Trudeau's congregation, had been founded by Adélard Langevin, an Oblate and archbishop of Saint-Boniface, whose own congregation had as its major goal the evangelization of the Aboriginal peoples. The sisters served as teachers in the schools and also provided domestic work in their role as auxiliaries to the Oblate Fathers. In both their evangelical and school work, the Oblate Sisters enacted the central ideas of redemption and salvation within a theological approach that construed the "Aborigine" as a "sad offspring of an ignored race," a "dreadful mixture," having "a useless, barbaric and often harmful life."[28] (A small number of Aboriginal and Métis women joined the congregations.) It would be fair to say that the Sisters of St Joseph were involved with First Nations children, in both residential and day schools, but the history is more complicated. The Sisters of St Joseph of Toronto is the mother congregation for five others: London, Hamilton, and Peterborough (and Sault Ste Marie which emerged from Peterborough, as did the Sisters of St Joseph from Pembroke). While the Sisters of St Joseph of Toronto were involved with First Nations education in British Columbia, it was Peterborough (in Thunder Bay), and Hamilton (in Cape Croker) that were involved with day and residential schools. (At least two First Nations women joined the Sisters of St Joseph of Sault Ste Marie, including two blood sisters who are Ojibway – sisters Eva and Priscilla Solomon.) As MacDonald points out in her chapter, the CRC submission to the Royal Commission on the Status of Women included the recommendation to increase rights for First Nations women, to phase out residential schools, and to respect the desires of the Aboriginal peoples.

Globality is a substantive property of the universal Church's historical process, while locality generates the shades and tones of the local Church; however, the link with the centre (the Holy See) cannot be neglected.[29] Particularly relevant to what happened after Vatican II are the series of informal and formal linkages, permanent or not, that bound sisters from various congregations; those linkages also bound male and female religious. The chapters in this book reveal the transnational dimension of the sisters' work – even when individuals carried out that work, as in the cases of Mary Alban and Alice Trudeau. Their work was itself immersed in networks that took the shape of structures.

Vatican II legitimized a movement toward redefining religious life, including the spaces in which to interact; consequently many sisters re-entered the world without fear of cognitive contamination and without fear of plurality. They did so on new terms, since Vatican II had already redefined the relationship with outsiders as one of dialogue and cooperation and called for an engagement with the world. Encounters with the world were not viewed – at least in many cases – from the position that the other was wrong. The new attitude generated a new form of globalism among members of the religious communities. Significantly, the new globalism did not consist of a common goal supplemented with some degree of alignment with the overall direction of the Church. Rather, it assumed a fragmented quality, exemplified by Mary Alban's biography and by the journey of Alice Trudeau. The new globalism was contextualized by the tensions the congregations lived as the personal intersected with the institutional.[30]

During the process of renewal and their encounter with the world on new terms, the congregations went through new collective and individual experiences as part of a metamorphosis of the Church at large – in the first two decades after Vatican II, but even in the preceding decade. To an important extent the change was reflected in a language that moved away from sacrifice, humility, reparation for sins, and obedience, to new semantic fields relating newly expressed emotions – fear of change, resentment, and happiness. Such a language represented a new way of being religious while crossing boundaries between the private and the collective, as was the case with the sisters' search for new selves. Vatican II's assertion that the sisters were members of the laity also accentuated a feeling of identity loss and a reason for questioning whether it made sense to remain in vowed life.[31]

The preoccupation with emotions and with the self is evident in the journey of Sister Alice Trudeau as a leader, as well as in some sisters' own recounting of experiences. Sister Mary Alban talks openly about her feelings when referring to her process of spiritual discernment of a new mission (Haiti). The submission by the CRC women's section to the Royal Commission on the Status of Women introduces a rights vocabulary to the subject of the education of women and First Nations women.

The demographic changes listed early in this introduction acquired a painful dimension when it became evident that those changes were leading in most cases to the "disappearance," as MacDonald states, of congregations. The material evidence is embodied in the closing and sale of convents. Sister Mary Alban, the protagonist of chapter 3, did not die in the motherhouse; the house was gone. The motherhouse of the Oblate Sisters is today a residence for seniors.

This book invites the reader to explore some of the most relevant historical challenges affecting women congregations, many of whom are disappearing, the Missionary Oblate Sisters being a case in point. Fifty years after Vatican II, and in the midst of processes in which residual elements from the past converge with the new geography of the Church, it raises the big question regarding women: *Where are Catholic women situated within the Church?* For some time now, women's congregations have been calling for a new awareness in all of us, insofar as we are all members of the earth community.[32] Pope Francis has addressed the issue clearly and strongly in his encylical letter *Laudato Si'* (On the Care of Our Common Home). But many of the issues that resulted in contradictions and dead ends in the renewal processes of the late 1960s and 1970s still remain, as do the silences of Vatican II and the hierarchical, gendered structures.[33]

1

Smaller Numbers, Stronger Voices: Women Religious Reposition Themselves through the Canadian Religious Conference, 1960s–80s

Heidi MacDonald

INTRODUCTION

In Canada in the 1960s and 1970s, Roman Catholic congregations of women religious (commonly called nuns) suffered a perfect storm. External social forces such as secularism, feminism, consumerism, the sexual revolution, expanding state initiatives in social welfare, and the Cold War seemed to be attacking them from without by questioning their relevance. The Second Vatican Council (1962–65), called in part to address the Church's response to these forces, initiated a period of profound self-questioning of women religious' customs, ministries, governance, and even dress. The often divisive congregational debates associated with the Vatican II era were sometimes perceived by women religious as attacks from within – within their own church and congregations. While many women religious welcomed the potential of Vatican II to allow them to realign their goals with the needs of the modern world and to enjoy more central roles in their church, they suffered greatly from the loss of both clearly defined ministries to the outside world and a secure understanding of their own purpose.[1]

Redefining their mission and reconstructing their collective and individual post-Vatican II identities further destabilized already struggling congregations. Between 1965 and 1975, the number of women religious in Canada fell 32 percent from approximately 66,000 to 44,127,[2] a proportionally greater decline than in the United States, where the number of women religious dropped from 179,954 to 139,225, or 25 percent in the same years.[3] This chapter will analyze how women religious, facing a downward spiral of membership and perceived relevance, used the Canadian Religious Conference (CRC) to reposition themselves in the two decades after Vatican II. Through the CRC, women religious joined their male counterparts in building an unprecedented national organization that pooled resources to deal head-on with human and economic resource deficits in their congregations, the threat of irrelevancy in a secularizing society, and a lack of influence on the patriarchal and hierarchical church at the local, regional, national, and international levels. Considering how women religious marshalled their voices through the Canadian Religious Conference complicates many assumptions about the decline of women religious in the post-Vatican II era. This chapter focuses mainly on the two decades following Vatican II because these were the years of greatest turmoil and consequently the period when the CRC worked most diligently and effectively to reposition the role of religious in Canada.[4]

SHIFTING ROLES

In mid-twentieth-century Canada, many provinces had strong Protestant and Catholic subcultures that had developed over centuries, and especially during the mid-nineteenth century when Ultramontanists insisted that "cross and crown" be completely separate, and that "cross" was more important. Ultramontanists lobbied provincial and colonial governments to allow social institutions, such as schools and hospitals, to be controlled by the Church. The Church could thus strengthen its relationship with its flock and impose certain values through these social institutions. These social institutions required a workforce, and several mid-nineteenth-century bishops invited congregations of women religious to operate schools and hospitals on behalf of the Catholic Church. It is not a coincidence that the highly effective and fervently ultramontane Bishop Bourget of Montreal focused his early episcopate on bringing male and female religious congregations to his diocese. Three French congregations of women religious accepted his invitation to serve in Montreal, and he helped found another four women's congregations, so that by the mid-nineteenth century, more than 1,000 sisters from ten different congregations served in Montreal Catholic schools, hospitals, and other social agencies.[5] This process was attempted and in some cases replicated in dioceses across Canada. The social institutions that were either founded or strengthened in this era continued to operate into mid-twentieth-century Canada. It was these very social institutions that were threatened by the mid-twentieth-century decline in vocations.

After growing steadily from approximately 10,000 at the turn of the twentieth century to 66,000 in 1965, the number of women religious in Canada began to fall. At the same time, the expansion of federal health care funding and the Quiet Revolution's targeting of religious education in Quebec led to less dependence on women religious and a consequent loss of status for women religious and their traditional work. Attrition, departures, and very low entrance rates in the decade after Vatican II reversed the long pattern of membership increases and threatened the future of religious life. By the end of the century, many of the 200 congregations of women religious in Canada had not received a single entrant for decades. Total membership had declined to approximately 18,000, the majority of whom were more than seventy-five years of age and retired from waged employment.[6] The decline threatened congregations' very existence with unanticipated economic, human resource, and identity crises.

It is somewhat ironic that Vatican II had invited the very renewal that seemed to spark falling membership. Several of the seventeen documents disseminated from the Second Vatican Council (1962–65) had encouraged a less hierarchical Church and a recalibration of priorities.[7] For example, the Dogmatic Constitution on the Church (*Lumen Gentium*, 1964) described the Church as a "mystery," and included the statement that, regardless of rank, all faithful were called to the "fullness of Christian life." Understanding that they could live lives equally devoted to Christ outside a religious order prompted some sisters to leave vowed life. Another key document, the Pastoral Constitution on the Church in the Modern World (*Gaudium et Spes*), proclaimed that the Church must be of the world, not separate from it, and that the Gospel must be interpreted in relation to the current world; *Gaudium et Spes* was also interpreted by some religious as discouraging the kind of religious life that separated vowed adherents from the people they served, which would have described a majority of pre-Vatican II congregations.

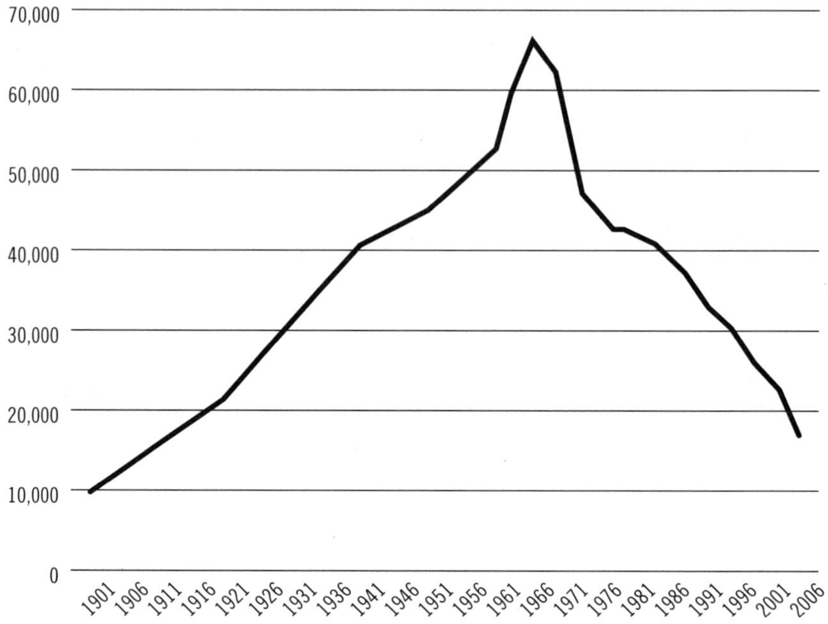

Figure 1.1 Number of women religious in Canada, 1901–2004. *Canada Ecclésiastique* (Montreal, 1887–1975); Lessard and Montminy, *The Census of Religious Sisters in Canada*, 353, table XLVI; CRC, "Statistics of the Religious Congregations of Canada," 1973–2004, A7, CRCA.

Religious congregations also had their own decree, Decree on the Adaptation and Renewal of Religious Life (*Perfectae Caritatis*). *Perfectae Caritatis* applied themes of Vatican II to religious institutes by requiring they "return to the sources of all Christian life and to the original spirit of the institutes and their adaptation to the changed conditions of our time."[8] Just as significant as the directive to adapt the original spirit of their foundings to the modern day, however, was that the entire membership was called to contribute to the renewal process. In the words of the decree, "An effective renewal and adaptation demands the cooperation of all the members of the institute."[9] A subsequent document, *Ecclesiae Sanctae*, explained that adaptation and renewal should be negotiated within congregations' general chapters, which were extensive meetings of delegates elected by all members of the congregation, usually held every four to six years (depending on the congregation's constitutions) to address congregational governance and mission. While in session, a general chapter represented the highest authority of the congregation, superseding mother superiors and other members of governing councils.

The special general chapters of renewal which *Perfectae Caritatis* set in motion, and which *Ecclesiae Sanctae* specified must start by 1968, were far more comprehensive than regular general chapters. Many congregations' chapters of renewal met for eight to ten hours a day, six days a week, six weeks or even more, and over two consecutive summers. The preparation was equally extensive: rank-and-file sisters participated in opinionaires, questionnaires, study groups, forums, and topical research committees, used to form proposals that were then voted on at the chapters of renewal.[10] Thus, not only was *Perfectae Caritatis* momentous in its call for renewal; its process of unprecedented, widespread consultation and rigorous debate was equally transformative.

Both the Church and religious congregations underestimated the impact of *Perfectae Caritatis*. The Vatican seemed surprised that North American and Western European congregations, long overdue for real discussions about religious life, not only accepted the Vatican's request for renewal but often exceeded its intentions. American theologian and Benedictine sister Joan Chittister wrote that the Vatican did not intend to set in motion such a large-scale renewal of religious life, but as women religious began to ask themselves what their responsibilities and essential character really were, they became excited about the potential for positive change: "Nothing went unquestioned: the nature of obedience; the function of the vows; the composition of the community; the place of authority; the character of ministry ... One loose brick toppled the entire system."[11] Historian and Sister of Charity Mary Olga McKenna also identified the renewal process as a turning point: "until the time of Vatican II, women religious were perhaps the most dependable but at the same time most expendable resources in the Church on the congregational, parochial, diocesan, and even global level."[12] After they had engaged in the renewal process, including by studying such Vatican II documents as *Lumen Gentium* and *Gaudium et Spes* and participating in dozens of self-reflective workshops, there was nothing expendable about them anymore.

Women religious voiced their concerns in the many opportunities offered within their congregations, and they also voted with their feet: one-quarter of women religious in Canada left their congregations in the decade following Vatican II. In the case of McKenna's own congregation, more than 400 of the approximately 1,700 members sought dispensations from their vows, a painful process replicated across North America with some congregations losing over 50 percent of members and only a small minority remaining unscathed.[13]

While the renewal process required by Vatican II was not the only reason women left religious life in the late 1960s through the 1970s, the opportunities to question and reflect were undeniably disrupting. The debates about the need for and degree of renewal affected all sisters, regardless of their perspective, and created factions within congregations. In the midst of the renewal and in the years to follow, many women religious decided they no longer belonged in the convent. Some felt pushed out, concluding that the renewed religious life offered nothing special to them anymore, or, conversely, some were disappointed that renewal did not go farther. Others were pulled by the variety of opportunities in the secular world – including careers, marriages, and relative autonomy – and the reduction in guilt that Vatican II had inspired through *Lumen Gentium*'s decree that the vowed life was *not* more valuable than the faithful life of a secular person.

Regardless of the various reasons women left religious life, their departure in large numbers created major challenges for the congregations they left behind, especially in staffing schools and hospitals, the two main areas in which women religious served until the late twentieth century. In fact, the number of sister-teachers in Canada fell by 74 percent from 1965 to 1975, from approximately 44,000 to 11,000.[14] The fall in the number of sister-nurses is more difficult to discern, but between 1970 and 1975 the number of Catholic hospital beds fell by more than 50 percent, from 60,954 to 26,356, as congregation after congregation ceded their hospitals to provincial governments.[15] In most cases, congregations did not have the human resources to keep up their former institutional commitments. This was further complicated by a boom in hospital construction in the 1960s, increasing expenses associated with modernized hospital accreditation standards, and increased wages connected to national hospital insurance. According to Eugene Vayda and Raisa Deber, the total cost of health care in Canada increased from $3.3 billion in 1965 to more than $11 billion in 1985.[16]

With regard to education, the greatest changes for women religious were in Quebec, where the Quiet Revolution's targeting of education discouraged congregations from continuing to administer schools.[17] For centuries, the Roman Catholic Church directed and administered education for its flock, arguing there was no such thing as secular education. Quebec schools were thus, in Ronald Manzer's words, "built on the rock of religion" and meant to reproduce generations of good

Catholics.[18] The election of the Lesage government in 1960, the Royal Commission of Inquiry on Education (Parent Commission) in 1961, and the forming of Quebec's Ministry of Education in 1964 shifted the focus from denominational schools (Roman Catholic and Protestant) to French and English schools and school boards.[19] The Lesage government modernized and secularized education in Quebec by taking it out of the hands of the Church and putting it firmly under state control at both the local and provincial levels.[20] Through increasing provincial educational standards for teachers, and strong secular teachers' unions, many women religious were pushed out of Quebec's mainstream educational system.

The Quiet Revolution, and most other provinces' milder versions of secularization, intersected with waning membership in many congregations and their recently redefined goals, which had grown out of *Perfectae Caritatis*'s appeal that congregations work more directly with the poor, decrease their focus on institutional work, and assign work based on individual sisters' talents and preferences rather than the needs of the congregation.[21] In other words, not only had membership declined and state control of education and health care expanded, but many remaining members of congregations were unavailable to contribute to institutional commitments because they were engaged in or discerning their new post-Vatican II role. Congregations that relinquished schools and hospitals did so not only because of government pressure but also because congregations or individual sisters decided to replace their institutional work with other work, including volunteer work serving the poor. If enough individual sisters discerned that they would no longer continue in institutional work – whether they stayed in the congregation or not – relinquishing that work became a foregone conclusion for the congregation rather than a decision consciously made by state or convent authorities.

Because of this layered context of falling membership; new congregational goals; new government mandates in education, health care, and social services; and frustration from the lack of recognition for their decades of service, there was no option for women religious other than to reposition themselves after Vatican II. The process, however, did not go smoothly. Most congregations suffered many painful years, redefining their goals and modifying their infrastructure to reflect the modern world through such Vatican II-encouraged initiatives as collegiality, subsidiarity, and respect for the individual, which all decentralized decision-making away from traditional church hierarchy to individual or local levels.

Two particular changes that came out of the renewal process – women religious' abandonment of the habit and veil, and relinquishing of a strictly common schedule – were often blamed for exacerbating declining status and membership in the 1970s. In fact, the context is more complex. Moreover, the pain within congregations is often underestimated. It is doubtful than any single woman religious – young or old, conservative or progressive – did not feel vulnerable during this period of instability. Neither could any congregation – large or small, founded in the seventeenth or twentieth century, French or English – not feel the weight of its uncertain future. Those whom the sisters served, including priests and bishops, were often also critical of the sisters' choices in their new roles, which caused further grief to the sisters.[22]

Discontinuing or greatly reducing their traditional institutional work in schools and hospitals, regardless of whether a congregation decided to do so or was forced to by provincial legislation or a lack of human resources, had a major impact on a congregation's identity and economic sustainability. Broadly speaking, relinquishing hospitals saved money, while relinquishing schools cost congregations a great deal, even though school funding varied by province.[23] Hospitals were often a financial drain on the congregation because of large capital cost requirements in buildings and technology. Patient fees were paid by the patients themselves (including through their health insurance policies) in most Catholic hospitals until 1958 when the federal government introduced the Diagnostic Services Act. These fees, calculated daily, were meant to cover a patient's meals and nursing care. Doctors' bills, tests, and medicine were separate but also the responsibility of the patient until the Medical Care Act was implemented in 1968, following Saskatchewan's model implemented a few years earlier.[24] Fundraising and donations were to fund the actual hospital building and equipment, and in Catholic hospitals the biggest donors were usually the sisters administering the hospital, who regularly put their salaries back into the hospital budget, or drew only minimal salaries.[25]

In the post-Vatican II era, membership losses made the specialized health care positions in Catholic hospitals much harder to maintain. Imagine a congregation that lost one-quarter of its sisters – and keep in mind that when they left, there was rarely a provision for giving notice; they left quickly and quietly. Sister-nursing staff, x-ray technicians, and pharmacists were impossible to replace quickly. Training other sisters took time, and even then there was the risk that the "replacements" might leave, too. The training was expensive and could take two years or more. Paying secular health care professionals was usually beyond the budget of most Catholic hospitals run by sisters. Catholic hospitals in Canada were dependent on the often-unpaid labour of women religious, and when that labour force contracted in the 1960s, the decades' – or even centuries' – long subsidization of Catholic hospitals was not sustainable. As Sister Stella MacDonald, a Sister of St Martha and the administrator of the Charlottetown Hospital, wrote in a quarter page guest editorial in the Charlottetown *Guardian* in 1975, "We never told you how difficult it is to keep patching worn out things and places … But do you, the public, have any idea how difficult it is to make a hospital designed 25 years ago meet present health care needs?"[26] Congregations across Canada withdrew from both large and small hospitals, often selling hospitals to provincial governments at greatly reduced prices, but prices they needed in their coffers as their membership declined and as it became necessary to consolidate loans on various buildings that, of course, they had not anticipated no longer needing.

Despite the very difficult economic situations facing congregations who ran hospitals in the 1960s, bishops and some members of the Catholic population were eager to maintain a Catholic hospital system parallel to the public (sometimes, unofficially Protestant) system, especially in the 1960s as the debate over the decriminalization of abortion raged; the average number of children born to Quebec women fell from 3.4 in 1960 to 2.0 in 1970 as a result of increased use of contraception and therapeutic abortions.[27] Catholic hospitals in Canada operated under an accreditation system that disallowed procedures that contravened Catholic moral theology and natural law, such as male and female sterilizations, abortions, and even some male fertility tests. While there were fierce fights to maintain Catholic hospitals, in more cases than not, these fights were too costly to win and more Catholic hospitals closed than remained open in the two decades after Vatican II.

State-funded Catholic schools faced less economic pressure than hospitals, but because the level of funding varied by province, some congregations did subsidize schools. Similar to Quebec, Newfoundland had a state-supported confessional school system beginning in the late nineteenth century, but unlike Quebec, Newfoundland's continued until almost the end of the century, which is largely why Newfoundland women religious (the Presentation and Mercy Sisters) were so determined to continue their work in education. Ontario, Saskatchewan, and Alberta had minority denominational separate schools that were also state-funded, with the exception of grades 11 to 13 in Ontario, which were only funded by the state beginning in 1984. The Maritimes had "gentlemen's agreements" whereby some schools in areas of large Catholic populations were unofficially Catholic and state-funded. Only British Columbia and Manitoba did not have denominational common schools, but in these provinces, congregations of women religious provided some fee-based Catholic schools.[28]

In provinces with separate school systems, including Ontario and Newfoundland, the Catholic system often paid teachers less, and women teachers in some provinces continued to be paid less than male teachers into the 1970s. Even if the congregation did own the school building, such a building was far less expensive to equip and maintain than a hospital. For these reasons, women religious did not usually rush to relinquish their schools in the same way they did hospitals. In fact, they often wished to stay in schools, in part because of the economic stability the sister-teachers' salaries provided. In the post-Vatican II era, religious made compromises about continuing in schools, including deciding to join professional organizations in Quebec.[29]

With approximately three-quarters of congregations primarily focused on teaching, provincial government salaries and later retirement pensions covered the bulk of operational expenses in most convents in the twentieth century. Sister-teachers' paycheques went into general coffers to offset the congregation's expenses for the many sisters who did not bring in a salary, including those in formation, in university, on governing council, retired, or in charitable/unremunerated work. This revenue also covered the basic needs of food, shelter, clothing, and post-secondary education for members of the congregation and also subsidized other works, including overseas missions. With some Canadian congregations having up to 3,000 members in the 1960s, operating expenses were huge. Major expenses were also incurred for buildings, not only, as mentioned above, for the schools and hospitals that many congregations owned but also for their own motherhouses and other residences. Significant debt from 1950s building campaigns complicated the situation even more. When entrance rates to religious congregations were at historically high rates in the 1950s, many congregations built new accommodations to house recent entrants. After Vatican II, declining membership required relinquishing these same buildings, and because most had been purpose-built as convents, they were often unattractive to buyers.

In the mid-1950s, for example, the largest English-speaking congregation in Canada, the Sisters of Charity, Halifax, built a 350,000 square foot, $7 million motherhouse to replace their motherhouse, which had burned to the ground a few years earlier.[30] Just a decade after the new motherhouse opened, 80 to 90 percent decreases in annual entrance rates meant not only that the congregation did not need such a large motherhouse, but also it did not have the revenue to maintain its $1 million a year expenses, including its $32,000 annual tax assessment. This financial crisis nearly bankrupted the congregation by the early 1970s, when no buyer could be found for the building and their collective teaching salaries had decreased 25 percent. The crisis was averted through a rigorous program of divestment of other properties, including several convents and two hospitals.[31] This phenomenon is most obvious in Quebec, which always had the majority of women religious in the country and where rural and urban landscapes are still dotted with former convents, many of which have been repurposed, often as post-secondary institutions, including CEGEPs.[32]

The withdrawal of sisters from traditional work in hospitals and schools and their transition into a wide variety of other work (including overseas missions, parish ministry, and paid and unpaid work with secular social agencies) – combined with selling off buildings, relinquishing institutional work, wearing secular dress, and living in smaller houses of often two to four sisters rather than in large convents – created identity crises in addition to the already-mentioned economic crises. Declining corporate identity intersected with losing their main recruiting base – schools – and decreased their potential for gaining new recruits. According to Patricia Wittberg, "Their institutional service [had] profoundly shaped both the public and private identities of the religious groups. Their 'success' was judged both inside and outside the Church, by the success of their institutions."[33] Moreover, "owning, running, and financing their sponsored institutions had provided an avenue to denominational power."[34] Losing their association with successful institutions prevented many congregations from attracting new members and decreased their leverage with the Church hierarchy.[35]

All told, the shifting roles of women religious and the uncertainty of religious life in general in the 1960s and onward required congregational leaders to seek new measures for venturing into uncharted territory and sustaining their revised positions in Canadian society and the Church. Before considering how they used the Canadian Religious Conference in moving forward, I first consider a view from the "outside" about the cause of decline in religious life.

THE IMPACT OF SECULARISM

The explanation for the falling membership and status in congregations of women religious that began in the 1960s is often given in one word: secularism. This argument states that the same issues that led so many individuals and families to stop attending church after the Second World War similarly discouraged young women from joining a religious congregation, or if they did join one, from having the "perseverance" to stay. In fact, secularism was just one of several 1960s social revolutions and it is unwise to uncouple it from concurrent movements such as the sexual revolution, the Quiet Revolution, feminism, and anti-authoritarianism. Most of all, because the secularization thesis has been criticized for its lack of nuance or application to lived experience, its application to declining membership of women religious should similarly be questioned.[36]

Secularization scholars have debated the causes and impact of secularism in the West, as well as its timing. In *The Death of Christian Britain*, Callum Brown describes a fairly crisp turning point in the 1960s and 1970s as thousands of people stopped going to church, and "this Christian culture of a common language, enforced as much by family and community custom as by law, fell apart."[37] Other scholars, most notably Hugh McLeod, have argued that secularization – or McLeod's preferred term, "dechristianization" – happened more gradually.

More recently, other post-Second World War scholars of religion, including Garnett et al., have shifted the debate "beyond church statistics and squabbles about chronology"[38] by proposing broader concepts of authenticity, generation, and virtue and evaluating post-Second World War religious adherence from within lived experience.[39] Brown, McCallum, and others in the new generation of secularization studies scholars nevertheless should be commended for considering the role of gender and youth in secularization, categories that are highly relevant to falling membership in women religious. It was, of course, the sharp decline of young entrants – seventeen- to twenty-year-olds – that most affected membership.

The secularization scholars, more focused on church going than on vocations, argue that women had a significant influence over whether their sons, daughters, husbands, and families attended church. As increasing numbers of women worked in paid employment, they may have preferred to spend precious weekend leisure time with their families rather than in church – a choice that affected their children, husbands, and families as well. These women's decision *not* to attend was less about rejecting their church and more about the scarcity of their free time. Other women were too frustrated with the Church's outdated moral teachings to continue to attend or to encourage their families to attend, as earlier generations of women had. Many Catholic women viewed the 1968 encyclical *Humanae Vitae*, which affirmed the sinfulness of artificial birth control, as the straw that broke their loyalty to the institutional Church. Both Brown and McLeod also consider youth agency, connecting 1960s youths' rejection of authority and insincerity to their decision to avoid the institutional Church. Their critics argue against single-issue explanations, however, and offer a more nuanced analysis, including an approach grounded in Charles Taylor's concept of authenticity, which reconsiders the subjective turn of the 1960s as more than a shift toward individuality. In Taylor's words, "for many people today, to set aside their own path in order to conform to some external authority just doesn't seem comprehensible as a form of spiritual life."[40]

My greatest concern with the secularization scholars is that they provide an abundance of correlations but still no proof of the *causes* of secularization. Lynn Abrams similarly argues that any attempt to explain "the relationship between women and religion, between feminism and religion, and between sexual activity and religion on a large scale ... tends to focus on the relationship between sexual activity and religion and to assume that this relationship must be a direct or causal one."[41] Abrams's effort at a more nuanced analysis uses oral interviews of mothers who came of age in the 1940s and 1950s and their daughters who came of age in the 1960s. Her sample is small, but she makes some valuable observations on the effect of intergenerational influence, saying that the "daughters were pursuing lives deferred by their mothers and in the process threw off the constraints imposed by the model of the good woman."[42] If Abrams is correct, 1960s mothers may have discouraged their daughters from becoming nuns. Whereas 1940s and 1950s mothers often perceived their daughters' entrance into convents as affirmation of the family's devoutness, 1960s mothers may have pushed their daughters to take advantage of the breadth of opportunities open to them; entering the convent may have fallen to the bottom of the list.

I would propose a possibility related to Abrams's argument: that the waning of Catholic institutions as early as the 1950s meant that far fewer Catholic children were exposed to nuns and priests, particularly in schools, and in the case of nuns, in hospitals. As Gilles Routhier has explained, the percentage of Quebec's teachers and various health care professionals who were men and women religious fell by more than a quarter – from 76 percent to 53 percent – in just fifteen years, between 1941 and 1956; Lessard and Montminy similarly note that the number of female novices in Canada declined 31.5 percent between 1940 and 1964.[43] Helen Ebaugh explains the same phenomenon in the United States by noting that the Catholic *student* population grew 200 percent in the 1950s while the number of women in religious congregations rose just 21 percent.[44] Wittberg's argument is also relevant: as women religious became less identified with hospitals and schools, they were less able to convey an identity, and in some cases, they *did not want* new members during this period of transition because they could not define their mission for potential members or offer them any security.[45]

The correlation between a proportionally smaller number of women religious – no longer distinct in their dress or work – and secularization seems just as relevant a factor in secularism as consumerism, an expanding social welfare state, the sexual revolution, or feminism. Put another way, would a child who had only sister-teachers for her first few grades and secular teachers thereafter not be likely to loosen her ties to the Church? The most commonly cited reason why young women entered religious congregations in the twentieth century is the influence of a particular sister-teacher. Fewer sister-teachers would surely mean fewer recruits, with a compounded impact over time. This is not to suggest that any one factor caused the decline in religious life but rather that there are more factors than some secular theorists suggest.

Related to secularization and decreasing numbers of sister-teachers and nurses is, of course, the expanding role of the social welfare state. The state's provision of more services formerly provided by the church weakened the bond of the laity with the church. But was state expansion a cause or an effect of the declining role of women religious? Did the state increase its role in health care and education because demand exceeded what women religious could provide once secularism had adversely affected their membership? The chronology is relevant. Because the number of men and women religious was already insufficient to sustain Catholic social institutions two decades *before* the 1960s, the inability of religious congregations to provide services to the growing population may have been as much a factor in the expansion of the social welfare state as the population's preference for care by the state rather than the Church. Again, because the result is not likely caused by a single influence, the variety of factors must be considered.

While women's religious vocations expanded steadily until the mid-1960s, the growth was not equal to population growth, and the ratio of sisters to members of the Catholic population in Canada dropped. Callum Brown has been justly criticized for overemphasizing the starting point of secularization and so the decline in vocations should be viewed over a longer continuum. The decline in vocations as proportionate to the population began in Canada in the 1940s, as it did in numerous other countries, including Germany and Poland.[46] In fact, it was the recognition of the insufficient supply of sisters that led to aggressive recruiting in the 1950s and early 1960s in Canada and the United States – recruiting strategies that did not, for a variety of reasons, produce entrants who, compared to earlier decades, tended to stay in religious life in large numbers. Attrition rates in religious congregations before Vatican II could be 50 percent or higher in the first three years of initial temporary vows.[47] There is some evidence that the aggressive 1950s recruiting strategies, which included the construction and operation of high school "aspirancies" for potential entrants, scaled-up discernment programs in Catholic high schools, and an explosion and revitalization of vocations literature that included passionate testimonials from the most photogenic of novices, yielded relatively few long-term women religious.[48]

If one considers entrants in the postwar to Vatican II era as experimenting with vocations in response to aggressive recruiting strategies, rather than making a life-long commitment, the post-Vatican II decline appears similarly less stark. That is, the hordes who left tended to be the most recent entrants who were the least attached to their congregations. Like their secular counterparts, they were not rejecting their faith as much as considering that there were other ways to live it out. In fact, Vatican II had encouraged them to live their faith in new ways, and their religious congregations and families were far less likely to tie their leaving to any failure in faith, morality, or discipline. As so many women religious explained in interviews, they left congregations after Vatican II because they were "freed up" from obligations.[49]

While more analysis is needed on why women religious sought dispensations from their vows in large numbers, there is no doubt that women's religious congregations were in crisis in the 1960s. Their membership was in a downward spiral, extensive discussions of renewal had created fractious debates in most congregations, and aggressive recruiting strategies were not producing long-term vocations. Women religious needed to regain some of their lost status or risk irrelevancy.

Figure 1.2 Women's Section, Canadian Religious Congress, 1954. Women religious at the first Canadian Religious Congress, 1954. © Canadian Religious Conference. Reproduced with permission from the Canadian Religious Conference.

In fact, one of women religious' main vehicles for repositioning themselves, their participation in the CRC, illustrates how secularization theorists' tendency toward abstraction misses examples of new models of faith that counteract the mere fading-away examples that some data demonstrate. Struggling to go forward in a destabilized environment, most Canadian congregations of women religious turned to the existing Canadian Religious Conference for guidance.

ROLE OF THE CRC

With few exceptions, congregations existed as islands unto themselves before the CRC was formed in 1954.[50] The leaders, also called major superiors, of all religious congregations in Canada were invited to attend meetings of the CRC in 1953. All professed members of their congregations were also considered members, and their congregations paid membership dues on their behalf. Intended to strengthen the network of the 186 religious congregations, three-quarters of which were female, the organization originally maintained separate men's and women's sections, each with their own executives, and focused on matters internal to religious congregations. The organization had a mandate to hold a national assembly at least every three years, but usually held them

biannually. These assemblies had nearly 100 percent attendance rates of congregational leaders, who valued the support and expertise provided through the assemblies.

Before Vatican II, the themes of the national assemblies of both sections reflected an internal focus with topics such as (for the women's section) "Religious Poverty in the Modern World" in 1959, and "Chastity" in 1963. In fact, when the women's section of the assembly addressed "The Health of a Sister" in 1957, it was only in the context of a sister's worth as a worker. Superiors attending the annual national assembly were told that it was their duty "to safeguard the health of their subordinates … A great capital has been put under their care: they must look after it, keep it intact and defend it."[51] Superiors were specifically advised to require a pre-admission medical exam, provide good nutrition in the convent, and allow 30-day retreats for middle-aged sisters at risk of burning out – all measures that assured a stable workforce and reduced the financial burden of caring for physically and mentally ill sisters unable to contribute to their congregation's work.[52]

The emphasis of the CRC in its first decade was on maintaining the congregations' workforce and empathizing with mother superiors who had so many jobs to fill, rather than the welfare of sisters. With teachers in such high demand as baby boomers entered school in the 1950s,[53] mother superiors were under pressure not to lose any sisters to illness.

In her address to the 1957 assembly, Mother Sainte Blandine, SCIM (Les Servants de Coeur Immaculé de Marie dites Souers de Bon Pasteur de Quebec), Sisters of the Good Shepherd, Quebec, explained: "It behooves major superiors to ensure oneness of action that will invigorate the great white army of religious in apostolic fields and infuse into the world the new elements of transcendental vitality of Mother church whose privileged children we have the honour to be."[54] The mother superior was underscoring congregations' obligations to the Church at virtually any cost. The archival documentation from the CRC in the 1950s does not suggest any attempts to change the status quo or give religious a larger voice in the Church, although they did express hope for better communications with bishops.

Immediately following Vatican II, the CRC became more assertive, proclaiming itself "the spokesman of religious life in Canada."[55] The CRC confirmed their new role through their general assemblies, which, while still very well attended, became more outward looking and more concerned with advancing the post-Vatican II roles of male and female religious. For example, the 1968 theme was "Community of Charity in its Relationship with God, One Another, and the World"; in 1972, it was "Spiritual Leadership," and in 1973, "Presence of Religious among the Less Favoured."[56] These provided guidance to leaders as their congregations' work shifted toward such areas as parish ministry and social justice. As such, the CRC encouraged congregational leaders to also be leaders in their perspective dioceses, in part replacing their institutional work with new work that the bishops and laity would see as equally valuable. The leaders of the CRC were broadening their purview, staking a claim to the broader Church and society. As they themselves reflected on the shift, they referred to their previous role as "limited," and claimed their new *responsibility* to provide the Church with answers "enlightened and unanimous as possible" on social and apostolic questions. The use of the word "responsibility" is significant not only in implying a tie to their vows but also in justifying their role as "spokesman of religious life in Canada." Through the CRC, religious defined and justified their new role in order to avoid having it assigned to them, particularly by bishops or laity.

The CRC executive recognized the immediate post-Vatican II era as a watershed moment. They understood that if they were to successfully lobby the very powerful Church hierarchy, absolute solidarity was essential. They parsed out their long-term objectives in 1968:

1 To make all religious in Canada keenly aware of the spiritual and structural renewal of religious life in Canada.
2 To inspire religious communities in Canada in their efforts to bring about spiritual renewal and an adaptation of their internal organizations.
3 To guide those in charge of formation.
4 To encourage solidarity a) among institutes regarding general principles, b) among major superiors by means of mutual support, c) within the CRC by the collective sharing of the responsibility for religious life and by the pooling of their resources, source material, specialists, and the like.[57]

These objectives envelop two crucially synergistic aims – encouraging congregations to engage in renewal, and building consensus within the organization – but ultimately there was one objective: developing a national religious life identity. If the CRC was to fulfill its 1965 proclamation to speak for religious life in Canada, their first three goals about renewal and the fourth goal on solidarity were critically interdependent. As discussed at the 1966 assembly, "religious communities have to become the most radiant, the most zealous laboratories of these new forms [of religious life] ... Some communities risk being left behind if they do not carry out at the opportune time courageous and necessary adaptations."[58] The CRC strategy was for religious congregations to accept a common understanding of renewal, and then, in solidarity, to present that understanding to the clergy, laity, governments, and even the general public as a *fait accompli*. At the same time that the CRC was educating others about the state of religious life in Canada, they were building a national identity for religious, educating bishops and the public about who they were. Implicit in this repositioning was a clarification of who they were *not*: identical, obedient, institutional workers. That educational program was the only way to save the more than 300 relatively unrelated congregations of male and female religious in Canada from obscurity.

With 99 percent of all women religious in Canada already represented by the CRC through their congregational leaders, the organization was an obvious vehicle through which the impact of Vatican II could be managed; its founding a decade before Vatican II and sixteen years before the start of the Quiet Revolution was highly fortuitous. The CRC was acting on its significant potential with 65,248 members in 1965. As the CRC executive focused on its target as "the spokesman of religious life in Canada,"[59] that potential power became actualized.

The CRC began to operate much like a union in the Vatican II era: their elected president became the one voice that spoke for the group to the Church hierarchy; members paid fees to be represented by the group and to benefit from collective negotiations; and fees were pooled to hire administrative support and experts who could address the challenges of the membership through research, advocacy, lobbying, and public relations – including, for example, by offering 34 different workshops at the 1976 assembly. The CRC reconstructed itself as a nimble organization ready to respond quickly to pertinent issues arising in the Church and society. They positioned themselves so that the Church hierarchy and the denominational and secular press would seek their opinion.

The CRC, which had always demonstrated elements of feminism, became more overtly supportive of women's increased roles in the Church and society by the 1980s. The increasingly assertive role of the CRC as "spokesman" of religious life was reflected in its larger administrative machinery. In the 1950s, the CRC had three departments – administration, publications, and continuing education – and just three full-time staff.[60] In the fifteen years after Vatican II, they grew to six departments with twenty-eight full-time staff. Like modern unions in the mid-1960s, CRC expansion targeted research and public relations, supported by a budget raised through annual increases in the mill rate from $0.20 per professed member of affiliated institutes in 1965 to $6.00 in 1976, which created an increase in the total annual budget from under $10,000 in 1956 to approximately $300,000 in 1976.[61] Most of the budget supported paid staff, who increased to twenty-eight full-time positions by 1979.[62] The CRC national office remained in Ottawa but the national assemblies were held in cities across the country, mirroring the opening of four regional secretariats – CRC-Atlantic, CRC-Quebec, CRC-Ontario, and CRC-West – with their own offices, staffs, and annual regional assemblies in 1964.[63]

It is notable that in Canada, male and female religious stayed together in one main organization, which kept their broad commitment to solidarity in religious life yet also placed special emphasis on feminist issues, such as women's right to hold leadership positions and to have access to all levels of education.[64] In contrast, Mary Henold has explained that American women religious founded three prominent feminist organizations in the United States – the Conference of Major Superiors (founded in 1956 and renamed the Leadership Conference of Women Religious in 1972), the National Council of American Nuns (1969), and the National Association of Women Religious (1970). The choice in Canada to build on an existing organization was strategic. Women religious may have benefited from joining their voices with those of their male counterparts. Stressing their commonalities as religious and underplaying their gender differences undoubtedly gave women religious better access to the Church hierarchy than they would have accomplished with a women's organization that risked marginalization and possibly suspicion.[65] Women religious were eligible to hold any office in the CRC; in 1969, the first woman president was elected, Sister Claire St-Amaud, Sisters of St Ann (SSA).[66] And because they outnumbered the male members of the CRC 3:1, the women religious were assured they would not be outvoted. Members of the CRC even voted to discontinue the separate male and female sections in 1972. The sections had been created out of "[concern that] the women would take a less active part in meetings which might have men as leaders." After sixteen years, however, the 1972 assembly minutes noted with humour, "there seems to be but little danger of this at the present time."[67]

RESEARCH ROLE

The CRC's immediate post-Vatican II expansion was motivated by their commitment to supporting congregations as they negotiated a new church and secular landscape. The president of the CRC, the Rev. Angus MacDougall, SJ, informed the assembly in 1964 that "the two disciplines that are going to influence society most … will be sociology and psychology. And therefore they have to influence the religious … If we neglect these areas we are going to neglect a very important influence on society."[68] Acknowledging the larger number of women compared to male religious, the first major project of the revitalized CRC was a census of every sister in Canada, organized by the CRC's newly created subcommittee on research. Through the CRC, congregations pooled their resources and applied theories and methodologies from sociology and psychology to the challenges facing them.

If the CRC was to speak for religious life in Canada, they had to know on whose behalf they were speaking. A census of their membership would not only define the membership but also shed light on congregations' most urgent need: vocations. While there had been a CRC commission on vocations in 1955, its goals reflected the organization's former aims. The new vocations study that began in 1964 showed the more sociological, professional, targeted, and determined approach of the CRC, which addressed vocations as a resource management issue.

Of the 197 congregations of women religious contacted about the census, 183 submitted completed surveys, representing 65,248 sisters, or 98.9 percent of all sisters in Canada.[69] That such a remarkably high response rate on a complex questionnaire was achieved in just three months shows the power of the CRC to achieve a collective goal. The preliminary census analysis focused on both the congregations' origins and on the sisters' backgrounds, including age, diocese from which they entered, current geographic location, and family of origin. This focus provided a baseline demographic analysis, unprecedented in its detail and national breadth. While congregations submitted statistics to their diocese or to the Vatican annually, depending on their governance structure, such statistics were usually limited to the total number of sisters in temporary and permanent vows and not tabulated beyond the diocesan level.

The 1965 census's national compilation of the number of sisters according to decadal age groups, father's occupation, and size of family of origin was revolutionary. That it was initiated and funded at a grass-roots level, parallel to rather than part of the Church hierarchy, was transformative for the CRC, which could now begin to discuss trends and help its member institutions plan for the future by recognizing the strengths and weaknesses in their congregations' membership and potential workforce. Highlighted findings included that six congregations had more than 2,000 members, twelve had between 1,000 and 1,999, and seventeen had fewer than 100. More than half of all sisters (over 35,000) served in the province of Quebec. The census further noted that the age range was evenly spread by decade between twenty- and eighty-year-olds, and that just under 3 percent of sisters were either under twenty or over eighty. A majority of sisters were from farm families and families with more than four children, suggesting a long-term dependence on Quebec-based agricultural families for recruits.

The CRC expanded the preliminary report with analysis aimed at "better understanding … the problems that can arise from all three of the following: the recruitment, the degree of perseverance, and the aging of sisters in the various groups of the various institutes."[70] These questions addressed how entrance rates and overall membership were shifting demographically. The data showed that rates of "perseverance" were roughly two-thirds for those who entered between 1940 and 1964, with the highest rates of lifetime commitment (83 percent) in congregations founded since 1940.[71] The emphases in the census show congregations' concern with declining membership and particularly how entrance rates were insufficient to meet insatiable demands.[72]

The CRC research department continued to make demographic analysis of members its main priority for the next two decades, tracking trends to assist congregations as they planned missions, budgeted for sisters' care, and prepared for mass retirements. An internal review of the CRC in 1972 had affirmed its earlier research mandate, noting that the organization's credibility depended on the quality of its research: "The CRC's credibility in the eyes of the [Vatican's] Sacred Congregation for Religious and for Secular Institutes, of the hierarchy, or religious in general, and of the public depends in large part on the seriousness that the CRC manifests in the area of research. Its leadership and its influence in shaping mentalities are exercised on this level as is its influence on the evolution of religious life, on the life of communities, on the involvement of religious life in the world of today."[73] For the next four decades, CRC annual reports included extensive – up to 40 pages long – biennial surveys and demographic analysis of male and female religious. Initially, the results were strictly meant for members of the CRC, but were released into the public domain within a decade. Sharing the thoroughness of the research conducted on their own membership was a deliberate effort at repositioning themselves in the 1970s as a thoroughly credible organization. In fact, deciding to share this particular data had multiple objectives.

The CRC's first statistical report released for public consumption explained, "We hesitated to publish the figures shown on the preceding pages and evermore so, to give their impact as shown in diagrams indicating such a decline. But, out of respect for the Christian message of which religious have for a very long time been the privileged witnesses, we had to sound a little warning bell that would alert the unthinking. We are living dangerously, seemingly about to go, without sufficiently preparing for the future."[74] Their acerbic use of the term "unthinking" was surely a reference to various priests, bishops, and laity who criticized them for their changing role. The CRC leadership was acknowledging what many – even some among their own membership – considered to be their failure to attract new members. They hoped that by publishing the bald reality of their statistics, the "unthinking" laity and bishops might finally understand the inability of religious institutes to maintain their pre-Vatican II institutional human resource commitments. As the CRC stated in 1973, the future membership of institutions could not be predicted because of "two unknown quantities, the number of entrances and the number of departures."[75]

The CRC's second statistical report, in 1975, noted disappointment with continuing decline, explaining, "The facts are not conducive to elation. On the contrary, we cannot help remarking once more how few are entering religious life, how many are leaving, and how age is creeping up on a great number."[76] This was not news to anyone in the CRC; their membership had been declining for at least a decade, and before that they were disappointed that the number of recruits was not higher. Making their decline public was a strategy to keep the loss on the agendas of bishops, laity, and the government. In 1977, the CRC stated that hope was fading that the drop in vocations was temporary: "The statistics repeat something we already know: the average age is higher, recruitment remains a distressing question and departures continue to challenge us."[77] The CRC was not so much admitting the unlikelihood that membership would ever rise again as informing the public of the reality that the role of religious in Canada would never return to its prominent mid-1960s levels. Subsequent statistical reports from 1979 to 2004 gave less commentary but continued to report on departures and deaths, as well as membership by age group, region, primary language, apostolate, and institute. The CRC discontinued their statistical reports in 2004. The data was time-consuming to collect, and they had long ago made their point about declining and aging membership.

The findings of the CRC on membership in religious life in Canada over four decades underscores the main need for the repositioning of women religious. The first issue is not just that membership rose and fell as figure 1.1 notes, but that the human resource issue was more complex. Figure 1.3 shows the number of withdrawals – also called departures or laicizations – since 1968. Peaking at more than 800 departures in 1972, the spike in the decade after Vatican II is clear. As the previous discussion has shown, it was not merely Vatican II but the impact of several intersecting factors that led to these departures. That the departures tended to be proportionately higher among the most highly educated members of the congregation further complicated how congregations planned their future work.[78]

Departures were not the only cause of decreasing membership, however. Figure 1.4 shows that when deaths are added to departures, the total loss of members annually increased from almost 700 in 1973 to 800 in 1983, and to 1,600 in 1993. Deaths alone decreased total membership nationally by 3 percent in 1973, 2.4 percent in 1983, and 6 percent in 1993.

Membership losses could vary by congregation, of course. Some congregations suffered heavy losses immediately following Vatican II while others had more gradual declines. Figure 1.5 shows examples from the membership of four congregations from four regions – the Sisters of Charity, Halifax, the Congregation of Notre Dame, the Sisters of

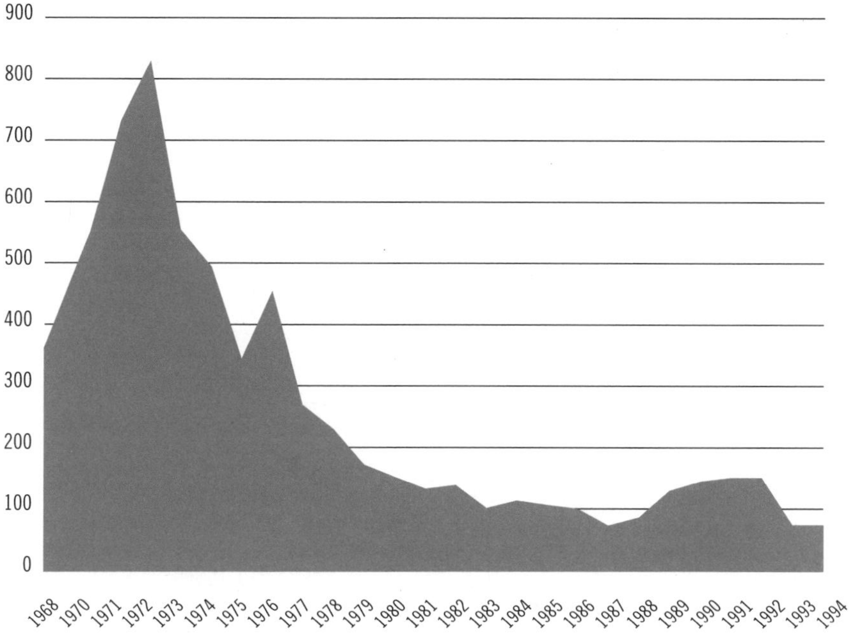

Figure 1.3 Number of withdrawals of women religious from congregations serving in Canada in selected years. CRC, "Statistics of the Religious Congregations of Canada," 1968–94, A7, CRCA.

St Joseph of Toronto, and the Sisters of St Anne – over four decades. The declines caused by both departures and deaths were relatively steady in these four cases. Data is not available for membership by region before 1996, unfortunately, but it was always highest in Quebec. The loss of almost 4,000 women religious in Quebec between 1996 and 2002 was larger than the total number of women religious in any other region in the same six years.

The post-Vatican II crisis in membership was caused by consistently low entrance rates. Until the 1950s, departures and deaths were balanced with new young entrants, but such was not the case afterward. Thus the dominant age groups in the congregations began to shift upward in the 1960s. By 2002, only 3 percent of women religious in Canada were under the age of 55, an age group that had made up 42 percent in 1973 and had been the majority until around 1970. Put another way, the average age was 47.8 years in 1965 and 74 years in 2004. This demographic analysis would not be available if the CRC had not created the data starting in the mid-1960s.

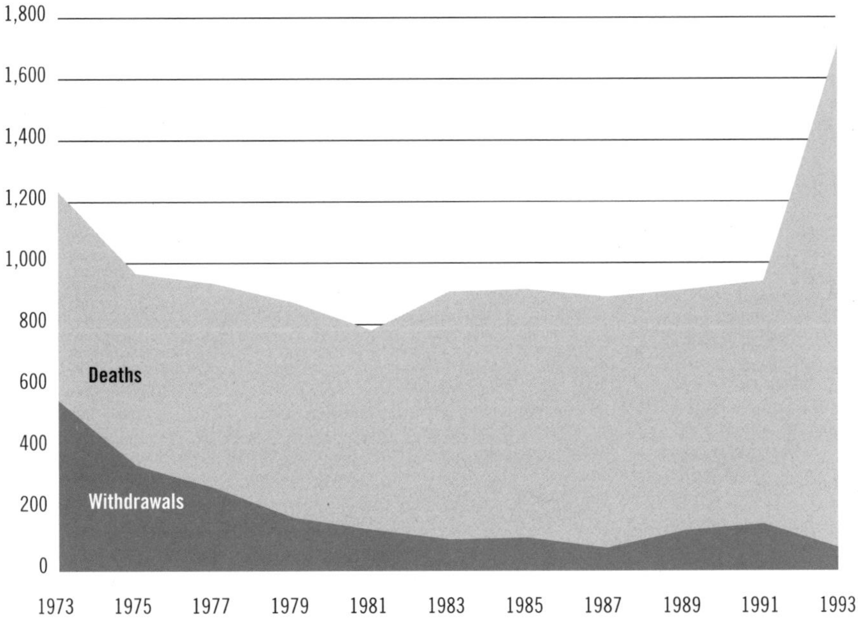

Figure 1.4 Number of withdrawals and number of deaths of women religious in Canada in selected years. CRC, "Statistics of the Religious Congregations of Canada," 1973–94, A7, CRCA.

The decision of the CRC to study vocations in 1955, the first year of their founding, to undertake a comprehensive survey using modern statistical and sociological analysis just as Vatican II ended in 1964, and then to publicly report on membership demographics in 1973 are all significant steps that demonstrate how the CRC constructed its post-Vatican II role and purpose. Vocations were always of the highest concern to the CRC. Not only did vocations represent the future of religious life, more vocations were constantly needed to keep pace with a growing population. Falling vocations were an indisputable sign that religious life was in decline. The CRC chose to learn as much as they could about the situation themselves in the 1960s, and then in the 1970s, once the trend was clear, the CRC made the data public, wanting not only bishops and the Catholic faithful to understand why religious could not provide the services they previously had, and even choosing to report the sociological phenomenon to the average Canadian through press releases to secular media. The CRC was repositioning itself in each

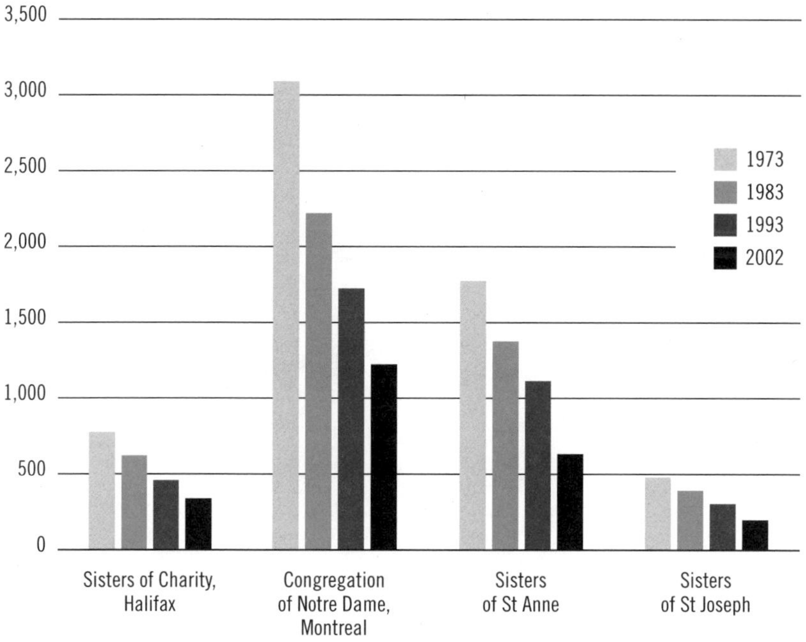

Figure 1.5 Membership of women in selected congregations, 1975–2002. Note: each column represents a decade. CRC, "Statistics of the Religious Congregations of Canada," 1973–2002, A7, CRCA.

of these steps and remaining loyal to its purpose as articulated in two of its long-term goals ("mak[ing] all religious in Canada keenly aware of the spiritual and structural renewal of religious life in Canada" and "inspir[ing] religious communities in Canada in their efforts to bring about spiritual renewal and an adaptation of their internal organizations").[79] Thus, in the immediate post-Vatican II era, the CRC ensured that even though women religious faced an uncertain future because of their declining numbers, they could still maintain an influence at the end of the twentieth century, inside and outside the Church.

LIAISON ROLE

After researching their own human resource issues, the CRC's second major goal was representing religious to other bodies. This was another key aspect of repositioning, but had also been a pre-Vatican II goal. In

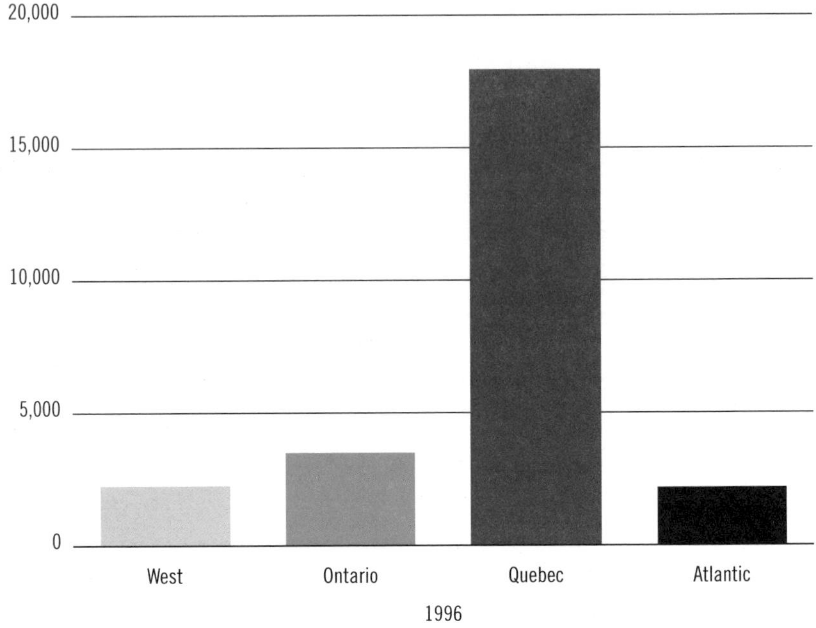

Figure 1.6 Number of women religious by region, 1996. CRC, "Statistics of the Religious Congregations of Canada," 1996, A7, CRCA.

fact, the most consistently reiterated goal of the CRC in its sixty-year history has been to improve communication between religious congregations and "ecclesiastical authorities." The greatest single strategy for improving communication was the CRC's lobbying of bishops on behalf of *all* religious. The first CRC national assembly meeting in 1955 identified the weakness of religious communities in communicating with bishops. The archival record does not elaborate on why that communication was so essential, but in a lacuna of formal structure between congregations and Church hierarchy, congregations were vulnerable to a "revolving door" of bishops who could randomly impose policies that affected religious and their institutional work.[80] Moreover, individual bishops were known to favour some congregations and disapprove of others; and congregations could receive a lot of support from one bishop and none from his successor. In designating itself "the spokesman of religious life," the CRC sought to become a vital bridge between Canadian religious congregations and "higher levels of ecclesiastical authority."

Good relations between bishops, who usually held a lot of power, and religious congregations, whose power was far more tenuous, became even more complex in the post-Vatican II era. Women religious were losing much of the influence they had amassed through their institutions and risked being perceived as irrelevant. Religious considered it essential that they be part of the discussion in the societal shifts that affected them, especially where provincial governments regulated their work. This was most seriously an issue in Quebec where the provincial government was asserting control over health care and education, which had previously been largely subcontracted to the Church. In 1964, the executive's report to the CRC national assembly described with great relief that successful meetings had been held with bishops concerning the conflict between Quebec's minister of revenue and religious congregations who were being asked to divulge financial records: "Thanks to this coordination of effort, some concessions could be obtained from the government of the province of Québec; it is hoped that still other concessions will be forthcoming."[81] At the same assembly, congregational leaders were told that the Joint Commission of Bishops and Major Superiors, which seems to have met infrequently and only at the request of the major superiors, had its "most outstanding meeting yet," and had put forward five resolutions to collaborate on vocations.

While the CRC reported these successes to its membership, it continued to work on the larger goal of a more formal structure of communication. In 1968, the CRC affirmed its goal as the liaison between religious congregations and ecclesiastical authorities, noting, "The CRC should be a rallying point and the instrument used by the superiors with a view to 'taking charge' of Canadian religious life, and that in a deep spirit of loyalty to one another."[82] It was implicit that this taking charge could not be achieved without the ecclesiastical authorities' recognition of the CRC as the spokesman for religious life. Like a union insisting on the value of collective bargaining, the CRC regularly reminded its members that solidarity was the best way to gain the bishops' attention and to ultimately have the bishops acknowledge a partnership, or at least an obligation to the CRC.

Four years after the 1968 reiteration of its liaison role, the CRC reworded its mission statement with an even stronger reiteration of its commitment to communicating with bishops: "The purpose of the Conference is to help its members in the carrying out of their role and of their functions; and to foster and maintain close collaboration of communities among themselves and with ecclesiastical and civil authorities in a true ecclesiastical spirit."[83] A revision of the statutes in 1972 added two new articles on "Liaison" and "Representation," which further underscored the CRC's role in representing all religious to ecclesiastical authorities.

Having so clearly defined this liaison role, the CRC jumped at the opportunity in 1975 to reply to the Vatican's invitation, through the Sacred Congregation of Religious Institutes (SCRI), to participate in a report on "Relations between Bishops and Religious."[84] The SCRI, surely acknowledging the power imbalance between bishops and religious in many parts of the world, asked four questions about what religious and bishops expected from each other, as well as about "concrete means to ensure ordered co-operation between [religious and] bishops and intercontinental, continental, national, and diocesan levels."[85] The CRC was delighted to appoint four superiors, one from each of the regional secretariats of the CRC, to be part of a committee that included four bishops who were also chosen regionally, and two officers each from the Canadian Conference of Catholic Bishops (CCCB) and the CRC. The parity of the CRC with the bishops was much appreciated by the CRC. An extensive report of the meeting in the *CRC Bulletin* explained its focus on repositioning the role of religious: "What is the primary concern to Canadian Religious is to determine what place is theirs by right within the Christian community and how they ought to carry out their mission ... Religious express the desire to be asked to take real responsibility and wish that the leadership of their bishops help to make the faithful become aware of the role that religious, both contemplative and active, ought to play within the Christian community, a role that may be frequently of decisive importance. By doing this, bishops will help promote religious life."[86] The CRC's frankness about their heretofore rights within the Church, as well as their challenge to bishops to promote religious life, were both central to the CRC's fundamental goal in repositioning religious in a particular way after Vatican II. They may have couched their desire in terms of asking bishops to help them explain the role of religious to the faithful, but in fact, the CRC wished equally, if not more so, for bishops to *appreciate* their role. The reminder that religious had a role "that may be frequently of decisive importance" was not something that all bishops accepted. And so the CRC's comment that more meetings were necessary between the CRC and the CCCB, and that meetings should include the subject of "the increasing role of religious communities, especially women's communities, in overall pastoral duties,"[87] were vital requests that the CRC had long waited to express.

Through the CRC's persistent advocacy, the CRC and CCCB held regular joint meetings by the early 1980s. The CRC remarked on the benefits of regular meetings, noting that one of their collaborations was that the CRC prepared the first draft of the CCCB's annual Pentecost letter.[88] That the CRC would note this as a "collaboration" either suggests that they did not mind being unacknowledged authors, as long as they were part of the process, or, alternatively, it may underscore the ongoing tenuousness of their relationship with bishops despite all their efforts to even out the power imbalance and gain a real voice with the bishops. The CRC and the parallel bishops' organization, the CCCB, certainly never became equal partners, but through the funneling of religious concerns through the CRC, the membership of the CRC – represented by almost 400 major superiors by the early 1970s – eventually gained the bishops' attention more than they ever could have as individuals. Collectively, in this way and in other ways, congregational leaders – formerly called "major superiors" – became more powerful, a successful outcome of using the CRC to reposition themselves.[89]

DISCERNMENT ROLE

While research and liaison were connected to the CRC's 1954 original founding goals and then accelerated in the post-Vatican II era, "discernment" was added in the 1970s and became a key part of how women religious repositioned themselves. This discerning, or "prophetic" role, indicated and insisted that as religious declined in number, their influence was not necessarily less significant.

As part of a review of its purpose and function, in 1972 the CRC Reassessment Committee recommended that the CRC "be accorded a role of discernment," specifying two aspects of the role, "prophetic" and "prudential":

> The PROPHETIC ASPECT consists in alerting religious to their proper role within the Church and society, which is a prophetic role, in the biblical sense of the term. This could consist in projecting the light of divine Revelation upon situations and problems brought to light by the sciences that deal directly with man;

> as also in witnessing … to the values of the Gospel in an authentic way that can be understood by the people of today.
>
> The PRUDENTIAL ASPECT can take various forms: evaluating experiments, working out a theory, discerning what is permanent in passing events, distinguishing true values from fads and infatuations, judging what is opportune and what foolhardy.[90]

This discernment role built on the CRC's main role as spokesman for religious life in Canada by claiming the special ability and *right* of religious to advise lay and secular society. Having ascertained their spokesman role, they further identified the subject on which they would speak. The CRC thus gave itself a powerful and influential role, putting itself on par with ecclesiastical authorities and secular experts. The 1976 national assembly, devoted to "The Prophetic Role of Religious Life," explained some of its preparatory documents: "The idea is to resituate religious life in a new social context … and to take a … look at the witness value of a religious life-style."[91] The CRC was carving out a niche for themselves as public advocates, using a strategy reminiscent of first-wave feminists who claimed their right to the vote based on their moral superiority compared to men. In fact, public advocacy was not a new role for the CRC, but became formalized in their 1972 statutes and as the focus of their 1976 assembly, through their self-proclaimed "special ability and right … to advise lay and secular society." An apt example of how women religious, through the CRC, had already exercised this role of prophetic discernment was in their submission to the Royal Commission on the Status of Women (RCSW).

Employing the same widely consultative process used in their statistical reports of membership, the CRC executive of the women's section responded to the call for submissions to the Royal Commission on the Status of Women in 1966. The executive sent a questionnaire to 240 major superiors soliciting content for the brief. Compiling the responses to their questionnaire led to discerning three topics for their submission: daycare for pre-school children, education in targeted areas, and "Indian and Eskimo women." The executive sought approval from the leaders of women's congregations with leading questions, including "Do you agree with the contention that, at present, the education of girls does not impart the necessity of continuing education for more than one avocation [marriage]?" Subsequent questions asked for more comments whether one agreed or disagreed.[92] After the questionnaires were returned, ten sisters met in Ottawa to draft the brief, which they then sent back to all the congregations for approval before making final revisions and submitting it in late 1968.

Accurate representation of how women religious could contribute was necessary, the president of the Women's Division explained, because she was "convinced that we must be prepared to implement whatever recommendations we make."[93] As with the renewal process of Vatican II, seeking all major superiors' consent to the recommendations made the process an important consensus-building exercise that solidified the participants' feminist principles. The CRC's brief justified the appropriateness of women religious' participation in the Royal Commission, saying they had "a definite right to express [their] opinions and to make recommendations regarding the general well-being of Canadian women."[94] They based this "right" on their education in a variety of fields as well as on their experience working with the poor, and especially women. They were, in effect, exercising the CRC's role as spokesman for religious life in Canada, and anticipating the role of prophetic discernment, which the CRC would formally embrace four years later. The forty-four-page submission of the CRC Women's Division to the RCSW made three main recommendations:

1. A thorough review of education departments in Canada with special attention to illiteracy and inner city issues; that the Department of Manpower provide women with equal job opportunities as men; and that special attention be provided for married and unmarried adult women (including immigrant women) for career preparation.
2. Free daycare for low-income women attending university and on a sliding scale for working women. (That daycare be considered as much of a right as education.)
3. Increased rights for First Nations women, including access to learning their own history; implementation of First Nations women development officers and social workers on reserves; the phasing out of residential schools while respecting the desire of the Indian people; and pre-kindergarten on reserves.[95]

During the preparation of the brief, the drafters raised education from the number two to the number one recommendation, ahead of daycare, which affirms Monique Bégin's argument that Canadian women's organizations became feminized through the process of drafting a brief to the RCSW.[96] Moreover, the accompanying nine-page appendix took a feminist stand on *why* women needed continuing education: "While the idea of the woman giving up her name and deriving all honour through her husband's accomplishments is taken for granted, this submerging of one's personality within another is a recognized barrier to testing mental health … A woman needs more than just a reassuring relationship with her husband and children. She needs a concept of self-acceptance and self-worth. If a woman cannot achieve this concept in the home, she must look elsewhere."[97]

Both recommendations echo Betty Friedan's writing in the *Feminine Mystique* regarding the "problem that has no name." Like Friedan, the women religious advocated meaningful work outside the home if women were unhappy as housewives.[98]

Then the CRC drafters of the brief took their feminist scrutiny a step further, raising the issue of women's ordination and female servers at Mass. While this was not in their main three recommendations, they included it as background material in the appendix, stating, "Another instance of a subtle prejudice can be found in the Catholic, Mohammedan and Jewish churches: women are not allowed to participate in the altar rituals."[99] The act of the CRC complaining to the state about the Catholic Church's lack of women's ordination or "altar girls" is revolutionary. It does indeed seem the CRC may have been among the women's groups in Canada who became more feminized in the process of making a submission to the CRC. The broad base of membership gave the executive confidence and power, as did drawing on their centuries' long experience in education in making the particular recommendations they did. From their perspective, they were repositioning themselves in a perfectly appropriate way, in keeping with their discerning/prophetic role.

The RCSW submission was completed before the CRC officially identified its prophetic and prudential discernment roles. Perhaps the positive impact of the CRC's submission may have encouraged the CRC to formalize its public advocacy voice. Of course, the role of women both inside and outside the Church was of keen interest to many women religious, regardless of the particular kind of feminism to which they adhered. Vatican II gave many Catholics – especially many women religious – hope that women's role in the Church would expand to include ordination and other opportunities. As women members of the CRC discerned their prophetic role, the status of women in the Church and society continued to be a priority for the organization, peaking, in many ways, in their 1984 national assembly theme: "The Role of Women in Society and the Church." That year, all of the CRC's quarterly bulletins were devoted to preparation for the assembly and each included long articles on promoting an expanded role for women in the Church and society from the perspectives of a bishop, a male religious, a lay woman, and a woman religious. Each addressed, among other things, the unfulfilled potential of women in the Church. In this vein, the women religious and their supporters continued to legitimize women religious' post-Vatican II discernment role. For example, in the first of the 1984 bulletins, a male religious reminded readers that women religious had been activists *before* the secular women's movement started:

> The experience of religious life, as lived in history, shows that women – and women's religious communities – have something to say about the role of women in the Church and in society ... The fact is that women religious did not wait for the women's liberation movement before managing individually, and collectively, to play a major role – as compared to the minor role traditionally assigned to them – in proclaiming and carrying out a Gospel which clearly involved promotion of human values ... [R]eligious were leaders in promoting such basic human rights as the right to life, to education, to health, etc. Long before Vatican II, religious women, unlike their usual portrayal on the screen or in the press, had acquired skills rare among women. They had attained a level of education and the competence which gave them the right to be considered full-fledged members of the present world's efforts to become more truly human.[100]

This short excerpt of Brother Jacques Berthelet's endorsement of women religious' post-Vatican II advocacy role is packed with details legitimizing that role. His emphasis on women religious' long experience promoting human rights, especially compared to their secular counterparts, affirmed their historic right to a role in public advocacy; they were there first. Berthelet's insinuation that secular women were more shallow in experience and interest – otherwise, why would they have so dispassionately "waited" for the women's liberation movement to form before noticing the absence of human rights in the world – added credibility to women religious by questioning their counterparts' commitment. Finally, his comment that women religious' historic roles have been underestimated further legitimized their post-Vatican II role by situating it along a continuum that included the long pre-Vatican II period. In sum, Berthelet's testimony contributed to women religious' repositioning in the post-Vatican II era by downplaying any newness and emphasizing the continuity of their work, a claim that suggested women religious surpassed secular women activists in human rights, and particularly gender rights advocacy. That a male religious and member of the CRC made this strong statement further confirms the strategy chosen by women religious to gain leverage through a mixed-gender organization for religious, rather than forming their own organization as American women religious did in the same era. The use of the term "human rights" rather than "the rights of women" adhered to the same broad strategy.

A final consideration of the CRC's strategy of repositioning themselves through their prophetic role is how they dealt with the abortion debate. In fact, this issue did not achieve consensus and therefore the CRC never took a public pro-life stand. The executive presented an appeal to the CRC from a sister connected with a pro-life group for a donation or endorsement, but the CRC instead instructed congregations "who chose to do so" to make contributions on their own.[101] Not surprisingly, the issue was raised several more times. Sister Bernadette, a congregational leader who belonged to the CRC, made an appeal in 1980 to the general assembly for a donation to the pro-life group Alliance for Life.[102] Some regional assemblies and individual congregations also voiced support for a pro-life stance. The Atlantic regional assembly noted their intention to draft a statement on the dignity of life for the national assembly; if they did approach the national assembly, the national assembly never reported it. Again, in 1988, two members of CRC-Atlantic expressed "surprise that no statement had been issued by the CRC at the time the abortion laws were struck down."[103] A 1983 article in the *CRC Bulletin* by Archbishop James Hayes of Halifax commented on the "importance of responsible sexuality" and noted that abortion was not just a women's issue but an issue for all, but he notably did not endorse the pro-life movement.[104]

That the CRC did not take a pro-life stance, despite some internal pressure to do so, highlights its commitment to both solidarity and a variety of feminisms. The CRC may have been hoping to avoid the controversy that erupted in the United States in 1984, when twenty-six American women religious, along with twelve priests and brothers, lent their signatures to a full-page advertisement in the *New York Times* that stated a plurality of opinion on abortion in the Church. The Vatican pressured the women's religious congregations to discipline thirteen women; eleven eventually recanted and two others left their congregations.[105] In Canada, the CRC avoided risking a break in solidarity by never taking an official pro-life stand.

While beyond the scope of this chapter, the work of the CRC continues relatively unchanged into the twenty-first century, providing networking opportunities and the power of collective action for approximately two hundred Canadian Catholic congregations of men and women religious. The need for the CRC continues in part because the Church remains a patriarchal and hierarchical institution without formal structures to guarantee women religious' voices will be heard. What has most changed, of course, is that the total number of women religious in Canada had fallen to approximately 10,000 in 2016, which is only 15 percent of the total number at the time of Vatican II. Biennial national assemblies, numerous committees, the tri-annual publication of the *CRC Bulletin*, and an effective executive and staff nevertheless negotiate and actualize the goals of the CRC. Restructuring in 2002 emphasized maintaining the CRC's "prophetic voice" and "respond[ing] to new challenges," with four services (formerly called departments): Communications, Mission/Formation, Priorités dans les dons, and Justice, Peace and Integrity of Creation (JPIC). A new mission statement, adopted in 2010, demonstrates both the continuity and evolution of the CRC since its founding in 1954: "The Canadian Religious Conference (CRC) is both a voice for and a service to leaders of religious institutes and societies of apostolic life. The mission of the CRC is to encourage its members to live fully their vocation in following Christ. The CRC supports its members in their prophetic witness to justice and peace within society and the church. The CRC looks for audacious ways of interpreting faith and life so as to embrace the new vision of the universe."[106]

CONCLUSION

Women religious did not need a national organization to represent them while they operated institutions and were praised for doing so. Administering all of their schools and hospitals had never been easy, but it was identifiable and respected work. Before Vatican II, women religious were, in many ways, the most essential workforce in the Catholic Church. They had power that they could leverage when necessary. In the post-Vatican II era, they risked irrelevance in a patriarchal Church that did not need them as much as it had before and that was nervous about any new role they might take on. Moreover, they were less visible due to their reduced numbers and their lack of a common uniform or corporate work. Through the CRC, women religious repositioned themselves, fighting strategically and effectively to have their relevancy recognized in a secular, post-Vatican II world.

2

The Missionary Oblate Sisters: Renewal and the Tortuous Journey of the Prophetic Feminist Vision of Alice Trudeau

Rosa Bruno-Jofré

The Missionary Oblate Sisters of the Sacred Heart and Mary Immaculate (MO), a bilingual (French and English) teaching congregation, was founded by Archbishop Adélard Langevin in 1904, in Manitoba, Canada. The foundation was Langevin's practical way of expressing his commitment to a culturally dual French-English vision of Canada, and of addressing his fears of Anglicization, which were heightened after the Manitoba government withdrew financial support for confessional schools in 1890. It was also a way to respond to the needs of the Oblate Fathers of Mary Immaculate in relation to the process of colonization of the Aboriginal peoples, mainly through the residential schools for Aboriginal children.[1]

Sister Alice Trudeau, a native of Manitoba, was superior general of the Oblate Sisters between 1981 and 1989.[2] Her prophetic vision went beyond the walls of the convent to embrace a new conception of the Church, and within it, of her community. The *longue durée* approach – traversing a longer span of time and even moving back and forth – employed in this chapter helps to capture the conjuncture generated by the Second Vatican Council (Vatican II) in her congregation and to tackle the divided reaction on the part of its members to that vision.[3]

I argue that the "failure" to enact her vision in the community moved her, along with Sister Cécile Fortier, to insert her work in a configuration where the boundaries were fluid and where she could freely live the radicalness of the Gospel – her spirituality as she understood it. The initial setting was the refugee camps in Zaïre/Democratic Republic of the Congo, after the genocide in Rwanda in 1994. I also argue that there is continuity between the principles of her vision expounded during her leadership and those in that new setting. I acknowledge, however, that the overall process was painful for Alice; it was not within the parameters of idyllic sisterhood.

In order to contextualize Alice Trudeau's vision, this chapter addresses the congregation's (The Missionary Oblate Sisters) complex process aiming at the resignification of vision and mission at the intersection of Vatican II (1962–65), the gendered and hierarchical qualities of the Church as an institution, the changes in the historical conditions of the congregation's apostolate that weakened their instrumental mission, and the encounter of the congregation with a plural world from a relativized position. Vatican II had changed the terms of the relationship with the world when it embraced modernity and defined encounters with other views and faiths as one of dialogue and cooperation. Under this new conception, the sisters were no longer to be perceived as upholders of absolute truth; neither were they any longer expected to renounce the world, but rather to be in solidarity with it. The interplay of new elements and a new language emerging from a belated discovery of modernity with the persistence of residual elements favoured by the limits encouraged via the institutional Church, I argue, helped to generate hybrid unstable meanings deprived of a central intentionality.[4]

In this chapter, Pierre Bourdieu's concept of "field," understood as a space containing a history, an internal logic, a symbolic capital, various positionings, and a network of relations, will be used to understand the configurations that developed among the sisters, as well as their discursive tensions.[5] I will analyze the congregation as a "field," a social space arena and a site of struggles during its renewal process. Also, the overlapping institutional and societal contexts, following Quentin Skinner's contextualist approach, will be taken as the frame of reference for understanding the meanings of the sisters' new utterances, the historical conditions of their actions – including fear of radical change – and the emerging intentionalities.[6] In addition, the concepts of "contexts" and "fields" will facilitate the examination of the "illocutionary

Figure 2.1 Fort Alexander Residential School, girls and sisters (Manitoba). Picture taken in 1916 on the occasion of a visit from Mother St-Viateur (Ida Lafricain). Father Geelen, OMI (front row left), was the principal of the school. Reproduced with permission from Sister Cécile Fortier, General Superior for the Missionary Oblate Sisters.

force" – the force derived from the conventions that determine what the thinker is thinking – in other terms, the intentionality, giving meaning, for example, to Trudeau's vision for her congregation.[7]

I complement the process of contextualization with Charles Taylor's notion of "social imaginaries" to explain the transition to a new way of being religious, and its limits. Taylor defines "social imaginary" as "ways in which they [people] imagine their social existence, how they fit together with others, how things go on between them and their fellows, the expectations which are normally met, and the deeper normative notions and images which underlie these expectations."[8]

For the historical analysis of this paper, I intertwine feminist theories and categories with one another in order to approach not only the complexities of power relations and patriarchy but also the gendered body of the sister as a component of Catholic identity formation, as well as the material dimension of place in the formation of subjectivities.[9] Concurrently, I treat the paintings and photographs presented in this chapter as signifiers of identity that reveal a bit of the sisters' understanding of their inner self and their community identity.[10]

Figure 2.2 Painting by Sister Marie-Immaculée, *La moisson d'or est offerte avec reconnaissance au Seigneur* (1954). Reproduced with permission from Sister Cécile Fortier, General Superior for the Missionary Oblate Sisters. Photograph by Beverly Wawruck.

LOOKING BACK: FOUNDATION, VISION, AND MISSION, AND CRISIS IN THE 1960S

On the occasion of the Golden Jubilee of the congregation (its fiftieth anniversary) in 1954, Sister Marie-Immaculée (Cécile Leclerq) painted *La moisson d'or est offerte avec reconnaissance au Seigneur* (The Golden Harvest is offered in Thanksgiving to the Lord), shown in figure 2.2. The sisters' mission in the Canadian prairies is conveyed here in the typical prairie scenery of a golden wheat field. The wheat sheaves are the harvest symbol of the Harvest of Gold, which signifies evangelization, the work in the prairies with settlers and with the Aboriginal children. However, there are no Aboriginal peoples represented on the land, only symbols of the presence of the colonizers (the metaphorical harvest). The landscape wilderness is tamed, and the land is farmed by the new settlers.

Archbishop Adélard Langevin stands with individual authority while the sisters are depicted as collective followers with little that distinguishes them from one another. The three sisters depicted are the first and second superiors general, Sister Ida Lafricain from Montreal and Sister Alma Laurendeau from St Boniface, Manitoba, who are honoured as co-founders, and Elizabeth Storozuk, born in Poland, one of the first sisters from Manitoba, who entered the convent in 1903 at the age of fourteen. The pictures of the sisters and Langevin were painted separately

Figure 2.3 Painting by Sister Marie-Immaculée (no title; Sister beside the river). Reproduced with permission from Sister Cécile Fortier, General Superior for the Missionary Oblate Sisters. Photograph by Beverly Wawruck.

and then tacked to the background. The artist, Sister Marie-Immaculée, wished to memorialize the foundation on the occasion of the fiftieth anniversary and keep the mission alive. Another painting by the same sister, shown in figure 2.3, memorialized the congregation's mission with the Aboriginal peoples; the setting is the surroundings of McIntosh Residential School, in Ontario, although the painting was done at the new motherhouse sometime in 1958. The painter portrayed herself and the sister who worked with her, Sister Marie-Arthur (Beatrice Trudeau), at the McIntosh Residential School.

The painting of the sister by a lake with an Aboriginal woman conveys what appears as an idyllic encounter with the Aboriginal peoples. One sister (Sister Marie-Immaculée) is taking a child's temperature and pulse, while the other sister plays with another child. The painting denotes that the sisters are needed. The sisters are starkly differentiated from the Aboriginals who are represented within this "wild" landscape, not in the farmed "civilized" landscape.

These images by Sister Marie-Immaculée, painted in the mid and late 1950s, signified the congregation's mission, their collective identity, a representation of the self as a community, and a historical memory. However, while the paintings hanging on the walls of the convent were a reminder of the sisters' mission and vision and their perceived success, by the early 1960s, the original instrumental mission regarding French Canadians and the Aboriginal peoples had been lost. The illocutionary force (the intentionality) – the salvation of souls of the Aboriginal peoples and the building of a Catholic order available to the settlers in the prairie provinces – disintegrated and lost the power to coordinate meanings of emerging experiences. The residential schools for Aboriginal children and forced assimilation were seriously questioned; it wouldn't take long to hear testimonies of sadness and abuse. As well, the process of redefining identity in the French-Canadian communities outside Quebec as a result of the break-up of the collective identity of French-Canadians in 1967 changed the political landscape. At that time, Quebec nationalists moved to self-determination and asserted that Quebec was the "national territory" and the "basic polity" of French Canada.[11] At the same time, the educational system had started to move in new directions, including consolidation of district school boards in Manitoba. The "long 1960s" (1958–74)[12] was characterized by remarkable economic growth, a boom that extended until 1975; the creation of the Keynesian state; and the emergence of a thriving middle-class, one that allowed for the creation of a consumer economy. In that period, Canada was shaped by demographic growth and immigration.[13]

These economic, political, and demographic factors had implications for education, the core of the Oblates' apostolate. As Hugh Stevenson puts it, "there was no thought of merely relying on the educational institutions which existed before the war."[14] The decline in the number of sisters – vocations had started to diminish in the early 1960s – added another layer onto the obstacles to full engagement in teaching. Between 1952 and 1963, the Oblate Sisters had 88 novices making first temporary vows, with an attrition of 13 members during this period. There was also an attrition of two sisters with final vows, and 13 sisters died. In the next decade, 1964 to 1973, 17 novices made their first temporary vows, with an attrition of 7, and an attrition of 19 sisters with final vows occurred; 19 sisters died.[15] On a positive note, the sisters had been able to further educate themselves. The 1963 report of the outgoing superior indicated that ten sisters had obtained a bachelor of education, 24 sisters a bachelor of arts, and 20 sisters had graduated from normal school at a point when the congregation had 278 professed sisters.[16]

Many sisters had been uncomfortable with a "symbolic universe" that could not integrate new meanings and experiences, not even those coming from Church organizations or from theologians to whose work they were exposed. While Superior General Jean-de-la-Croix (1951–63) attempted to deny the changes taking place around her and remained firmly rooted in the past, the Oblate Sisters, together with members of other congregations, attended courses on Scripture and theology taught by Sulpician professors at Saint-Boniface Major Seminary.[17] The sisters became familiar, from the late 1950s on, with the work of theologians who are considered precursors of Vatican II and were involved in connecting the Church to the modern world – Karl Rahner, Henri de Lubac, Yves Congar, and Jacques Maritain, among others. A new conversation began – in the case of the Oblate Sisters, along the hallways of the convent. In the official records of the congregation, however, its vision of spirituality had become frozen in time, due to external attachment to rules, obedience to the superior, and a notion of mission that, by the early 1960s, had become de-aligned with the context of their apostolate and the movement of the Church itself.

During the Second Vatican Council, in particular the autumn of 1963, the sisters attended informational meetings on church renewal, the nature of the Church, and the need for a dialogue with the world. The new superior general, Jeanne Boucher, was appointed that year. A liberal theology friendly to modernity continued to flow. The sisters realized that they had to embrace the world – a world that they had previously learned to reject and be suspicious of – and even to assume an active role in exercising judgment. However, it wouldn't be easy to move away from their dualistic worldview.

The process of re-envisioning that opened to the light with Vatican II was framed by internal contradictions: the sisters' preoccupation with self-development, inner freedom, and healing; persistence of residual elements – attachment to what were perceived as sources of respect and authority; conformity with the notion of working within the boundaries of the institutional Church; fear; and the emergence of transformative visions like the one expounded by Trudeau. The limits set by the Catholic Church itself after the movement toward change and *aggiornamento* set by Vatican II became an important point of reference in the various understandings of the new reality. A new field emerged during the renewal and re-envisioning process. It encompassed a difficult journey on a fractious path and imagined futures that were not to be.

Sister Ghislaine Boucher represented the celebration of the hundredth anniversary of the congregation in 2004 in a painting (figure 2.4) that she thought was inspired by the Holy Spirit. She interpreted the

Figure 2.4 Painting by Sister Ghislaine Boucher, 100th anniversary of the congregation in 2004. Reproduced with permission from Sister Cécile Fortier, General Superior for the Missionary Oblate Sisters.

past in light of the imagined future, which she saw as consisting of lay people carrying on their mission.

The artist believed that the Holy Spirit guided her in this endeavour. She wanted to express symbolically the life experience of the Missionary Oblate Sisters' congregation and the inspiration that guided them through their hundred years of existence. She explains her painting:

> The history of the MO congregation unfolds on planet earth, against the backdrop of sea and sky evoking the cosmic dimension of the Sisters' mission in time and space under the power of the Holy Spirit and the loving guidance of Jesus and Mary.
>
> To the left of the painting, the Virgin Mary is leading the Founder (Archbishop Adélard Langevin) and the co-founders (Ida Lafricain and Alma Laurendeau), followed by a long line of Oblate Sisters and lay people (students, collaborators, and associates) to fulfill their educational mission represented by the open book on lower right.

> Mary appears transfigured in her ethereal-looking white robe, as she is joyfully treading lightly, the icon of the Wisdom of God, leading the dance of the universe as the first of the redeemed (as described in the Book of Sirach 1: 1–10).
>
> The large cross at the centre with the white broken host at its crossbeam releases a gushing torrent of life-giving water flowing to the right, bringing fertility and growth to a variety of luxurious vegetation.
>
> This represents Christ's offering of himself for the life of the world. From the wounded side of Christ gushes forth the gift of the Holy Spirit, portrayed by the white dove and the long multi-coloured rays of light (the seven gifts and the charism of the Congregation).
>
> The whole panorama is laid over a red heart-shaped background symbolizing the tremendous love of the Sacred Heart of Jesus that permeates and transforms all Creation.
>
> The multi-coloured rays of light shining obliquely across the centre of the painting create an effect of translucence and an impression of warmth, evoking the active presence of the Spirit and the openness and transparency of those who yield and respond to God's loving plan of life in abundance for all.
>
> Finally, the bold contrast of colours, lines, and shapes create a provoking picture of life, energy in motion, and power, which evoke the supra-human love and activity of God, empowering the fragility and weakness of his children in co-creating and transforming the world. The painting envisions a legacy being carried on by the lay people.[18]

The painting expresses a new vision and meaning, and a utopian understanding of the future. However, the documents and oral histories provide us with a different story: a complex path of difficulties opposed to reaching a common intentionality – that is, against generating a force to coordinate meanings emerging from new experiences.

Walking for a moment from 2004 back to the preceding decade, we notice that the leadership reflected the contradictions and fears that emerged through the process of change. In fact, the 1990s conveyed a crisis of the congregation's collective identity in light of recent changes and visions and, in particular, of Trudeau's vision (superior between 1981 and 1989). The leadership of the 1990s embodied a challenge to the previous transformations, a desire to look for protection in the past, retrenchment. This positioning had gained ground along with the persistence of old socialized norms, ways of doing things, and fear engendered by the limits set by the Church, yet in hybrid combinations with some changes. But there was also another positioning in the field, a grassroots movement within the congregation that had assumed the visionary insights that questioned memories and historical narratives, spiritual dualism, patriarchy, Foucauldian "normalization" of emotions, and traditions. As well, the experience of change had generated a language of justice and women's spirituality, along with a spirituality of love for the cosmos in a divided field in which the interplay of forces did not favour the deployment of a central intentionality informing the congregation's vision and mission. The decline in the number of sisters did not help; neither did the institutional boundaries (that were to be defied by Trudeau during her tenure as superior general from 1981 to 1989). Furthermore, in an age in which multiple modernities were opening their way to a postmodern age of fracture, the sisters encountered a plural world where different worldviews interacted – Catholicism being one of them – in a relativized context and a relativized positioning after Vatican II. They also encountered a historical reality in which collective purposes and meanings had been fragmented in multiple identities in their North American society, in which the market had become the central force. Congregations were part of that world now.

In the year of the centennial, 2004, Sister Alice Trudeau died (of a stroke) in Nairobi, Kenya, on 27 October. She was cremated in a Muslim cemetery, the only crematorium in Nairobi. Some of her ashes were buried in a Catholic cemetery in Nairobi and the rest in the Oblate Sisters lot in St Boniface. Trudeau and Fortier had been on a special mission in Goma, Democratic Republic of the Congo, and Burundi (and in general in the Great Lakes Region) for nine years since 1995, as invited by the Institut de Formation Humaine Intégrale de Montréal (Institute of Integral Human Formation). They had worked with the project Appui à la Reconstruction de la Personne (Aid to the Reconstruction of Persons, ARP), giving sessions based on the process of "actualization of vital human strengths" to caregivers and educators.[19] Trudeau and Fortier worked with non-governmental organizations (NGOs). They lived their spirituality in a secular organizational context, despite the presence of sisters from various congregations as well as male religious involved in the project. How did these two sisters reach this point? How is this mission read in the context of the history of the congregation and in relation to Alice Trudeau's vision for her congregation? I try to answer each of these questions in the following sections.

THE RENEWAL PROCESS, BOUNDARIES, AND THE PROPHETIC CALL THAT COULD NOT BE

The Report to the General Chapter of July 1963, submitted by the outgoing superior general, Sister M. Jean-de-la-Croix, was still grounded in a hierarchical, authoritarian understanding of leadership. It still paid close attention to the Directory and the Manual of Practices, which had been revised following the way of the co-foundress, Mother Marie-Joseph du Sacré-Coeur (Alma Laurendeau). However, times had changed. The superior expressed regret that "in our houses, there is no time to study our Rules. We would find, in these wise counsels [from the co-foundress] aimed at bringing about uniformity in our lives and at giving our religious family its particular characteristics [*sic*]."[20] Attachment to rules – an integral part of a Catholicism based on rites, prohibitions, observances, and permissions – continued to be stressed by the superior as the means to spiritual perfection. The outgoing superior had not gone along with the efforts of other congregations to respond to changes; neither had she shared information and documents coming from the Canadian Religious Conference.

The denial of change had generated great discomfort in the congregation at a time when it was losing both its instrumental mission and consensus on the intentionality behind its vision and mission. Consequently, when the sisters elected Jeanne Boucher superior general (1963–73, a time the sisters would later define as *therapeutic*), the congregation eliminated obsolete customs and structures of common life built upon observance of rules; and the sisters took back secular names, modified the habit, and soon moved to secular clothes. The leadership model under Boucher changed from pyramidal to a model known as the "through" in which relations with authorities were not defined. Alice Trudeau was then a young sister. Notably, the congregation held the Chapter of Aggiornamento (1968) and drafted the *ad experimentum* constitutions, entitled *Witnesses* (*Témoins*), later approved by the General Chapter in 1981 and by the Roman Congregation for Consecrated Life in 1983.

During the 1960s, the congregation had configured a field characterized by emphasis on the exploration of the self while trying to figure out a way to a common intentionality. It is fascinating to observe that, despite being imbued for many years in the anti-modernist culture advocated by the Holy See before Vatican II (even as the Church herself had engaged with modernity in many ways), the sisters tried to embrace the components of modernity *as a cultural project*: the autonomy of the subject, the self-assertion of the self, and the expansion of discourses of creativity, reflexivity, and discursivity in their lives. For example, during the 1960s and 1970s the congregation was intensively engaged in workshops and courses on human development and the search for a reconstituted relationship with God, taught by Father André Rochais and his teams, and known as Personality and Human Relations (Personalité et Relations Humaines, PRH). The leaders of the congregation, Boucher, Boutin, Tétreault, and Trudeau, all went through the processes of PRH. Rochais (1921–90) was a French educator who had been influenced by Carl Rogers's work, in particular *On Becoming a Person*, and who had developed his own guidelines for personal analysis.[21] Central notions in PRH included persons' growth to their full potential, acknowledgment and search of the subjective, and seeking existential freedom. PRH aimed at discovering meanings within oneself; listening to one's self-experience and finding direction from within; looking into oneself with open eyes to develop unity and harmony; being aware of one's felt experiences (sensations); distinguishing between what one says about oneself (knowledge) and one's sensations; and having a relationship with God.[22] The overarching goal was to live in personal harmony and to be true to one's conscience.

Nevertheless, as Delanti puts it, modernity entails the experience of fragmentation: "the sense that modernity as a social project destroys its own cultural foundations."[23] Certainly, the sisters in most congregations had a difficult time reconstituting their social imaginary as a community while moving away from uniformity and external rules.

The contribution of readings that appealed to the sisters and influenced the change in outlook and their personal journeys cannot be disregarded. The sisters became familiar with feminist literature, in particular with Betty Friedan's *The Feminine Mystique*, as Sister Dora Tétreault recalls, the first feminist book that reached some of them. As Heidi MacDonald, who includes the convent as a site of transmission of feminist politics, observes, some of the recommendations made by the Women's Division of the Canadian Religious Conference to the Royal Commission on the Status of Women (begun in 1967 and reported in 1970) echoed Friedan's *The Feminine Mystique* regarding the "problem that has no name." MacDonald writes: "Like Friedan, the women religious advocated meaningful work outside the home for unhappy housewives."[24]

Friedan gave some sisters critical insight into the situation of women in the Western world and into how destructive the suburban dream was. Women's personal, isolated experiences could also be understood as political and collective experiences. Why did Friedan's book become so appealing to some sisters? It did so because it questioned the role assigned to women by patriarchy – a role that women were convinced to see as desirable, even as their own identity was left aside, thus stunting growth and perpetuating the mystique; later, Friedan would question the process of ascription of the role itself.[25] Some sisters could identify with these elements of identity due to the role and status assigned to them in the Church. For these sisters, the book was also a window into second-wave feminism.

In the 1960s, a number of the sisters, particularly transformative leaders Dora Tétreault, Lea Boutin (later superior of the congregation), and Alice Trudeau, had become familiar also with Teilhard de Chardin (some of the sisters even took courses on Chardin's theories at Marymount College, affiliated with Loyola University in Los Angeles). Particularly appealing were Chardin's notions of how God's creation worked through cosmic evolution, the development of human consciousness as leading to greater individuality, and his vision of a potential for unified common consciousness of humanity.[26] As well, during the 1950s and 1960s, many sisters, in particular those who led the process of change, had been exposed to Emmanuel Mounier's (1905–50) personalism which Tétreault interpreted as a "new concept of the person and as person engaged with the world."[27] Mounier envisioned a new social order, a new worldview that moved beyond collectivism and individualism to embrace personalism and communitarianism in social relations.[28] Tétreault thought of Mounier's vision "as awareness of the self, that we could have freedom and rights and exist in our own right in the community."[29] Tétreault also indicated that some sisters, including herself, Boutin, and Trudeau, had started to embrace the idea that they would not be able to grow spiritually unless they became morally and intellectually autonomous persons.[30] This understanding converged somehow, in the process of renewal, with Karl Rahner's and Yves Congar's ideas with which many sisters had also become familiar. According to those ideas, the Bible needed to be interpreted in the light of anthropological and biblical research as well as in light of the configuration of religious life and in dialogue with the world. But even more, the sisters needed to deconstruct the normalization and control of emotions ("depuration of emotions") that set constraints to the relationship with the world, with other people, and among themselves. Most sisters were open about this need. These were important components of the emerging field in the early renewal process.

Under the leadership of Sister Lea Boutin, superior general from 1973 to 1981, the congregation started to build a new circular/participatory model of governance with the superior at the centre, as part of the process of renewal. (Trudeau was a member of the General Council during Boutin's second term.) However, it seems that many sisters did not have a sophisticated formation needed to work toward a new common vision. The Acts of the 1977 Chapter indicate that there was a new realization that it was necessary to move the emphasis from the self to projects of community rebuilding.[31] The search for personal identity and development had generated a degree of fragmentation and neglect of a common spiritual life. This realization was also a factor when Trudeau brought her vision of change to the community. The Acts state, when dealing with community life, that "Our community life in the local groups suffers from lack of communication, dialogue and even sharing at a simply human level; more serious, at the spiritual level, there is lack of sharing around the Word and lack of dialogue at the profound levels of faith [*sic*]. Accordingly there is disaffection and lack of mutual trust that leads to criticisms and infantile comparisons."[32]

The Acts of 1977 continue to point to the need to return to the sources, in particular "to deepen our communitarian devotions in light of the Gospel, the Vatican Council II, and the directives of the Founder [Langevin]. The next revision of our Constitutions should take into account more closely our spirituality and our spirit of reparation in relation to the problems of the contemporary Church."[33] Using as reference *Evangelica Testificatio*,[34] the Chapter recommended deepening the relationships with God through the spirit of prayer, and both personal and community prayers as a way to live their oblation. It recommended using George A. Aschenbrenner, SJ's, daily "Examen of Consciousness" method to develop deeper conscientization and discernment. As evidenced in the Acts, the language of the 1970s does not convey a preoccupation with the woman religious searching for her identity.[35] Instead the Acts report problems with alcoholism and drugs, letting the reader infer that the disintegration of the autocratic pillars sustaining a notion of community generated problems among some of the sisters.[36] In line with the need to generate a process of communal participation and discernment, the Chapter also approved the creation of "community life projects" in each local group of sisters. It is important to note that the superior general reported that in 1974 Tétreault offered a session organized by the Canadian Religious Conference (CRC) entitled "Evangelization: Christ, the Man of the Beatitudes" and that twelve sisters had participated in sessions on community discernment offered by the CRC Women's Division.[37]

Sisters Tétreault and Boutin tried to rediscover the original inspiration for the congregation, following the directives of *Perfectae Caritatis*, which stresses the relevance "that institutes have to their own particular characteristics and work. Therefore let their founders' spirit and special aims they set before them as well as their sound traditions – all of which make up the patrimony of each institute – be faithfully held in honor."[38]

There were historical conditions of reception that would affect the reading of *Perfectae Caritatis* and that had an impact on the tense emergent field that the sisters began to configure.[39] The sisters tried to balance a critical questioning of the past with the acknowledgment of a legacy that legitimized their own existence. Their renewed spirituality had, of necessity, to relate to the founder and to the spirituality he gave them, relate to Vatican II documents (in particular *Gaudium et Spes*),[40] and relate especially to the Canadian Conference of Catholic Bishops. Thus, the congregation moved toward embracing social justice and eventually the option for the poor (in line with the documents from Medellín, Colombia, and Puebla, Mexico).[41] This is an important link to Trudeau's transformative vision.

The sisters, going back to the original instrumental mission, had created a conceptual and historical link between contemporary engagement with social justice and Langevin's struggle in his large diocese of St Boniface for the rights of Catholics and French Canadians at the end of the nineteenth century and the beginning of the twentieth.[42] The peculiar, historically anachronistic connotation of the link was due to the fact that it was difficult to connect the new referents of the concept of social justice (especially in the long 1960s and 1980s) with the founder's fight for the rights of Catholics and French Canadians within the context of the colonization of the Aboriginal peoples, the needs of the settlers, and his questioning of a liberal project that could affect Catholic interests. It is not surprising that from the late 1970s on, there was a search for a new language that conveyed the congregation's renewed spirituality, one that would ground their vision and mission – a language that took various meanings in the congregation following standpoints regarding change. Tétreault, who had written a number of documents for the congregation, particularly in the late 1970s, 1980s, and 1990s, abandoned the language of pain. She qualified that language as masochistic; she led the congregation to shift from a language of mortification and grace to a language of social justice, although vaguely defined.[43] As well, *reparation*, central to the congregation's spirituality and identity, was re-signified from a cloistered, contemplative notion of reparation for offences against God (not only by the sisters, but also by the world, by sinners). To fulfill the old notion of reparation, the sisters would pray day and night, fast, and perform many kinds of sacrifices to atone. As Sister Lea said a few years later, in a conversation in 1994, the idea of reparation came from a theology of atonement and redemption.[44] Tétreault remarked in this exchange that "with the new theology, social justice being one of the elements, the notion of reparation moved from a vertical dimension to a horizontal one, and hence became restoration, transformation, and growth. The new notion embraced the understanding that people were wounded, and that it was necessary to repair (heal) the woundedness in all."[45] The new theology took as its starting point human experience, keeping the evangelical notion of poverty quite central. The sisters explained that the new understanding was different from the thought of a God that had to be appeased.[46] The reinterpretation began to be elaborated during the time of Lea Boutin with research support from Tétreault. It became a component of the configuration of ideas of the new field that was emerging and providing context for the process of renewal, the space in which Sister Alice Trudeau would later try to articulate and convey her vision.

The new context influenced the re-signification of mission and the sisters' ministry, branching out from teaching in Catholic, public, and residential schools for native children to a variety of ministries that acknowledged the sisters' personal inclinations and talents. Thus, at the end of Lea Boutin's tenure in 1981, there were only thirty-three sisters in the teaching profession (compared to fifty-seven sisters teaching in 1977); other sisters were involved in pastoral ministry, spiritual direction, reflexology, secretarial work outside the congregation, nursing in hospitals and in the congregation's infirmary, working with the mentally challenged, and working with the deaf. One sister was working as a technician in the audio-visual department in a college; there were sisters working in Africa as catechists and to promote the status of women (a new dimension of their mission); there were sisters who were library technicians; there were also sisters taking care of their elderly mothers. The understanding of mission had clearly expanded; in 1977, the Chapter had already moved toward a "revalorization" of their mission as educators, emphasizing their role as educators of the faith while grounding their new understanding on a re-reading of their first constitutions. Indeed, in the first constitutions (1906), the founder had written that education meant showing Jesus and moulding Jesus (in the hearts of the children), and that the sisters were educators of the faith.[47] The new constitutions approved by the Chapter in 1981, and by Rome in 1983, redefined the sisters' role as missionary educators: "The principal objective of the congregation is education in all its forms."[48] Article 5 of the new constitutions defines their role as educators of the faith as follows: "In all our apostolic activities we seek wholeheartedly to collaborate with the family, the Church and society in developing a Christian vision of life, liberty, and justice among young and old."[49]

Patricia Wittberg advances a very helpful thesis to account for the tensions permeating the configurations of ideas taking shape in the new field and the building of a renewed social imaginary. She argues that after the collapse of their ideological frame, religious congregations developed defence mechanisms that prevented them from addressing the problem.[50] Among the self-defeating patterns Wittberg mentions are vague charism and/or mission statements including various interests in the congregation; emphasis on personal growth and development of the members, reflecting a tendency to interpret community in terms of the needs of the members; work as individual projects, spirituality as private; and the near impossibility of developing and sustaining communal commitments.[51]

Wittberg's theory partly explains why, following the collapse, the social imaginary supporting the community would be rather unstable. Congregations would have to deal with dispersed working and living arrangements that did not favour communal commitment; the commitment mechanism – living and working together, protection against the outside world, limited contact, shared sacrifices – could not be used any longer to sustain an outdated model of religious virtuosity taken from the seventeenth century.[52] As Wittberg writes, the new congregations founded in the nineteenth century reflected the retrenchment that took place in the Church in the aftermath of the French revolution and the rise of liberalism, and the Church's condemnation of modernism. Within that context, women's groups in particular had adopted cloistral restriction and outdated spiritual ideologies. It was therefore difficult for women's congregations in the second half of the twentieth century, especially those without strong theological foundations, to transition from a model grounded in a concept of obedience that ignored fundamental tenets of Western liberal democracy, without an account of egalitarian issues, topped with an understanding of chastity and poverty that was not touched by Freud and Marx, to an alternative contemporary model of religious virtuosity.[53] Religious life had been out of sync with the Western world; the encounters were not comfortable even as the interactions with the social milieu through the congregations' apostolate had generated various engagements with the historical conditions of the time.

During Sister Lea Boutin's tenure as superior general, a number of sisters took courses in theology and pastoral studies and continued reading Karl Rahner and Yves Congar (Tétreault attended Congar's courses at the Dominican College in Ottawa during the 1978–79 academic year). Tétreault, Trudeau, and other sisters took courses on social justice and Christian basic communities in Latin America, and read Gustavo Gutierrez and Leonardo Boff, among others,[54] becoming familiar with liberation theology in a more systematic way. Notions of social justice and the option for the poor would take root among a group of sisters. A strong prophetic positioning, having as illocutionary force social justice and the needs of those suffering, developed within the field during the leadership of Alice Trudeau, superior from 1981 to 1989.

In the 1980s, feminist theology reached the congregations, opening a new understanding on the gendered politics of the Church, and leading eventually to an inquiry into the production of the sisters' own subjectivity as women religious and to a critique of dualistic theology. Sister Lea, after her tenure as superior, completed a doctorate in ministry at St Michael's University in Toronto. In 1991, she published *Women in the Church: The Pain, the Challenge, the Hope*, in which – using as central categories women's experience and praxis to critique patriarchy – she questioned the language and ideology sustaining sexism, racism, and classism, all of them structural components of patriarchy. The assumption that the masculinity of God-language is not a cultural or linguistic accident, she wrote, makes patriarchal domination common sense and ordained by God. She also urged, following Thomas Berry, the move to an all-centred approach to theology, and, in line with ecofeminism, to nature-centredness. The influence of Elizabeth Schüssler Fiorenza is evident in her writing.[55]

ALICE TRUDEAU: THE GROWTH OF A VISION AND THE INVISIBLE BARRIERS OF POWER AND FEAR

Following her superior's (Lea Boutin) recommendation, Sister Alice Trudeau left teaching in 1976. She took a one-year Ignatian formation program in spiritual direction at the Jesuit Institute of Formation in

St Louis, Missouri, followed by a thirty-day retreat in Manresa, Spain.[56] She served as a member of the General Council from 1977 to 1981, while serving as director of Saint Charles (one of the congregation's houses) where she also founded the St Charles Retreat Centre. The centre reached out to lay people, women and men, looking for spiritual growth. Trudeau organized and coordinated Ignatian Spiritual Exercises with Jesuit fathers Fernand Bédard and Luc Guérin.

Trudeau's early visionary insights on spiritual development were not fully shared by her community, as implied in one of the few personal notes she left. She wrote that she had a hard time with the new ministry and that she felt alienated, rejected, and hurt. However, she also went through inner healing and reflected that she grew in freedom and in love.[57] That was when Father John Main introduced her to Christian meditation, which she would adopt as her preferred form of prayer. As discussed earlier, in the late 1960s and 1970s, Sister Alice had adopted the Rogerian approach that she, along with the other sisters, learned through Rochais; she later used it to support her Ignatian spirituality. She now reflected that the non-directive and subjective approach – listening, mirroring back, and clarifying – conveyed by Rochais's programs had become her way of interacting in a helping relationship. She believed that a person who becomes conscious of her feelings and emotions can change her behaviour.[58] However, she also noticed that in the process of changing, individuals became narcissistic, losing sight of their own means and personal resources, and that she did not have the tools to help in those situations.[59]

Sister Alice Trudeau was elected superior general in 1981 and re-elected for a second term for 1985–89. In 1981, the congregation had 208 professed sisters of whom 207 had perpetual vows and only one had temporary vows. The decline was clear. Lea Boutin's report as outgoing superior contained a comparison of 1981 with 1 June 1977, grouping the sisters by age; see tables 2.1 and 2.2.[60]

The process of renewal and the search for a vision happened at the intersection with the aging of most established religious congregations, and soon with the prospect of their own "disappearance," a term coined by Heidi MacDonald.

Trudeau moved further by advocating a renewed form of spirituality displaying a set of pillars that sustained a peculiar configuration of influences, interpellations, and intuitions, and nourished a new positioning among members of the congregation. We can think of the congregation at the time as a "field" in which positions opened way to relations of force. Trudeau's spirituality was grounded in her emphasis

Table 2.1 Sisters by age compared between 1977 and 1981

AGE	NUMBER OF SISTERS IN 1977	NUMBER OF SISTERS IN 1981
25–34	2 professed temporary 5 professed perpetual	0 professed temporary 4 professed perpetual
35–44	0 professed temporary 40 professed perpetual	1 professed temporary 27 professed perpetual
45–54	33 professed perpetual	32 professed perpetual
55–64	53 professed perpetual	48 professed perpetual
65–74	52 professed perpetual	46 professed perpetual
75–84	36 professed perpetual	32 professed perpetual
85–94	10 professed perpetual	18 professed perpetual
Total	**231**	**208**

Note: In 1981, the median of the congregation was 63 years, and the average 63.54 years.

on women's experiencing of spirituality, and her concern with the relationship between faith and social practice. Trudeau was always trying to get in touch with her inner self as a woman religious, something that the institutional culture had not favoured. Her questioning of the place of women in the patriarchal structure of the Church, like that by many other sisters of the time, started very early and was deeply intuitive. When reflecting on her feminism, she recalled in 1994, "But I always had a feeling for women. Even with Vatican II opening many doors, I recall as a religious beginning to ask myself: is there a place for women in the Church?"[61]

Trudeau did not have a strong theological basis, nor was she concerned with epistemological issues to be resolved; but she was very receptive of the work of feminist theologians such as Mary Daly,[62] Rosemary Radford Ruether,[63] Sandra Schneider,[64] and later, Elisabeth Schüssler Fiorenza[65] and Barbara Fiand.[66]

Trudeau was aware of the limitations of the Rogerian approach for inner healing, although as superior she continued to promote Personality and Human Relations workshops – aiming this time at empowerment

Table 2.2 Annual decrease in sisters between 1977 and 1981

YEAR, ON 1 JUNE	DECEASED	LEAVING	NUMBER OF SISTERS
1978	6	0	225
1979	2	3	220
1980	7	1	212
1981	4	0	208
	Total diminution: 23		

Note: On 1 June 1977 the congregation had 231 sisters.

and at an understanding of the personal rhythm of growth. She also encouraged care of the body, something that had actually started with Sister Lea: therapy, spa, massage, reflexology, shiatsu, and so on, as well as holidays. Trudeau promoted a holistic vision of prayer and the person, which Sister Rose Marie Viallet described as a new way of seeing the human body; it was not only the spirit and the prayers that were important.[67] "They [Lea and Alice] were ahead of their time."[68] The liberalization of the body was important to Trudeau in terms of breaking with a pervasive dualism that made the body a source of sin and moving to an integrative approach.

In 1977, Trudeau accepted an appointment mentioned earlier, the directorship of Saint-Charles, Manitoba, a community house with twenty-one sisters that Trudeau would change into a retreat-centre, where she organized thirty-day retreats in cooperation with a team of directors and two Jesuit priests. She started group journeying with lay people for thirty weeks through St Ignatius Spiritual Exercises in Daily Life. (Later, when Alice was elected superior general, Sister Dora Tétreault became coordinator of the program, which transferred to the motherhouse and expanded and flourished for ten years.)

Trudeau also brought to her leadership as superior a will to challenge what she perceived as unjust – that, as well, was nourished by her feminism. This took concrete shape in 1983, when, as superior general, she made a presentation to the national Congress of the Oblate Fathers and actually denounced the oppression suffered by the sisters under the authority of the Oblate Fathers and the priests.[69] She had consulted with the sisters and in her presentation she quoted these sisters' experiences, feelings, and also their visions of future work. Trudeau made the case that the role assigned to the sisters as auxiliary to the clergy in the missions and parishes placed them under the authority of the clergy and at their service, a subordinating role. This role was characteristic of the time; however, as she pointed out, there were disadvantages inherent in it, and even abuses that the sisters had experienced because of it. Consequently, the sisters were made to see themselves as inferior and were not motivated to develop their autonomy or to take initiatives or to assume responsibility. Immaturity was thus encouraged. Some sisters were resentful, Trudeau said, because they felt used and exploited. She further added: "Without question, it is necessary to say that the sisters did not have, perhaps, the courage to confront the Fathers, assert themselves, and make their needs known."[70] She also made the case that because the salary arrangements made verbally – between the sisters' founder, Archbishop Langevin, and the congregation when the sisters went to Cross Lake in 1909 – were never revisited, the sisters lacked the financial resources for ongoing education. Furthermore, the salaries for the work in the residential schools were inadequate.[71] In 1979, the fathers had decided to provide the sisters a sum to send a sister to a spiritual retreat in recognition of past errors, but it did not amount to much.

Given the absence of a strong theological basis, Sister Alice Trudeau's vision was not theoretically articulated; yet it had great coherence in its praxis. It was sustained in her profound intuition and in relation to an imagined community. It constituted embodied thinking (a sense of things) and looking for a practical way to change the archetypical character of Church ideology and theological tenets. In her presentation to the Oblate Fathers, Sister Alice referred to renewal. In the last years, she said, her congregation had gone through a process of renewal, a re-foundation of the Institute: "It is not men anymore who preside over this re-foundation, but women, the Oblate Sisters. We, women, took over this job and we should make personal and community choices to orient our future toward a solid revitalization that will enable us to further increase our service, not to the clergy any more, but to the people of God and the Kingdom. For this, we had and we still need the help from the masculine congregations, and in particular from the Oblate Fathers."[72]

It is significant that she suggested a move to a reignocentric (kingdom of God) approach, away from service to the clergy.

In the same presentation to the Oblate Fathers, Trudeau argued for her vision of the woman religious. In her view, the woman religious

Figure 2.5 Oblate Sisters launching the new constitutions in 1983. This photograph is in candid style, capturing a moment in the discussions of launching the constitutions in 1983. The sisters represent themselves here in lay clothing, immersed in dialogue around a table, which communicates values of shared governance and inclusivity. Pictures of chapter deliberations during this period reveal a world of women spontaneously reconstructing their own roles within the organization. (Thanks to Ana Jofré for her input.) Reproduced with permission from Sister Cécile Fortier, General Superior for the Missionary Oblate Sisters.

was in the process of moving from a status of subordination to one of equality, co-responsibility, and complementarity. Within this linguistic context, she argued, the definition of "auxiliary to the clergy" was also in the process of changing – and so were its practical implications. In her words, "Eve is going to find her place beside Adam." For this, she said, it is necessary that reconciliation and integration take place in each of us between the "animus" and the "anima," the masculine and the feminine in our being. Trudeau spelled out her approach by taking concepts from the controversial and conservative theory of integral complementarity (women and men were created equal but different and with complementary roles, with male headship in the Church and family), although she gave it her own eclectic twist. It is necessary, she explained, "that we acknowledge that we are not in opposition but in complementarity, that we learn to dialogue, to know each other and welcome each other with our richness and weaknesses of being." She called her audience to discovery: by means of a joint concrete apostolic project – that is, a joint pastoral project whereby each could contribute, in an attitude of constant mutual opening, but only what each is capable of contributing.

In her presentation, Trudeau also shared some positive experiences of dialogue, common search, enriching confrontation, and co-responsibility, in the movement from an authoritarian pastoral agency to one based on partnership. As for the difficulties that sisters encountered, she mentioned priests' decisions that were against the "gait" of the pastoral team; priests' emphasis on money and administration; priests generating distance from people; their planning without consultation; their tendency to assign tasks; their lack of interest in spiritual renewal; and their indifference to prayer, among others.

Of particular relevance in her interpellation was Trudeau's vision of the Oblate woman in the Church and the world. She portrayed the Oblate woman as *Porteuse de Vie* (Bearer of Life), setting the frame of a complementarity approach with biological and psychological essentialist components, while at the same time questioning control and hierarchy. She called on the priests to share authority. That call was courageous in her context; but theoretically speaking, the argument appears trapped within the boundaries of patriarchy, even as she attacked the social organization of the Church as signifying relationships of power.

Trudeau stated that she envisioned the Oblate religious encouraging lay people to live their role as baptized, to live the "priesthood of the baptized." She also made it clear that she did not see the role of the priest – as pastor of the Christian community and principal celebrant of the liturgy of the sacraments – as superior to that of women religious or lay people. The problem here is that she was not fully cognizant of the power relations involved. Her speech read, "I too must give Christ to my brothers and sisters, and help them to live of [*sic*] His life." She went on to say that she could be an instrument of reconciliation while a priest presides over the celebration. This is what happens, she said, with spiritual direction: "How many times I have heard confessions and I have been the instrument that God used to prepare a person to celebrate the sacrament of forgiveness?" On the matter of celebrations, Trudeau also quoted an Oblate sister (anonymous), who said that the Church had become a Church of sacramentalization, often removed from evangelization and from pastoral work among the marginal, the poor, and the dispossessed; that the Church often celebrated signs that had lost meaning and were related to a reality that people have not lived; and that the priest had become the man of the sacraments. People went to the priest to negotiate, said the nameless Oblate sister, to demand the sacrament, while the woman religious became the assistant in the preparation and celebration of the sacraments. So Trudeau made the point that at the source, in Jesus's life, there is little mention of the sacraments, but Jesus talks a lot about the oppressed, the little ones, the unfortunate, and all those in need to whom he showed great compassion and took concrete action to help; Jesus was always ready to help victims to get out of their misery. Those were the reflections that nourished Trudeau's notion of social justice – a notion with deep spiritual content, and a notion that she tried to make central to the life of her congregation. This approach to social justice is central to understanding the force coordinate of her vision.

Later in her presentation to the fathers, Trudeau referred again to the vision that two Oblate sisters had conveyed to her regarding the future of the pastoral parish, in which the Church of tomorrow is composed of Christians truly engaged in building the Kingdom of God, the new world as Jesus wanted it. For that, the priests and the women religious should be seen as equal to other Christians and be among the people, serving one another. Trudeau quoted Paul's call for each disciple of Jesus to be a living member of the Church. She then quoted another Oblate sister who had made the point that women and men are equal and different, from which she derived the importance of both the masculine and feminine element participating in the Church and in the world. Notably, at that point Trudeau did not question gender construction.

In summary, the characteristics Trudeau envisioned in joint pastoral work are the pillars characterizing her vision, as well as that of the members of the congregation supporting her. She wanted a change in the way of naming the religious: instead of "Father/Sister," and "Oblat/Oblate," she chose "priest," "lay," and "religious." And since co-responsibility calls for redistribution, a new way of sharing authority, and an opening to diversity, she wanted to reposition women religious and lay people. As a sister had told her in relation to her own pastoral work,[73]

> In this Church-Communion, the clergy, without ceasing to make decisions, will have to invent structures for communal decision-making with the faithful; without ceasing to teach, there will be much to learn; without ceasing to preside over the liturgical life, they will not be the only ones to celebrate. This new vision of

> Church justifies for all Christians an adult, responsible participation. The initiatives can come from above or below, from inside or outside the visible frontiers of the Church, from the most alarmed believer to the members of the hierarchy.

In Trudeau's vision, this new mentality requires that the Church forget the distinction between lay people and members of the clergy; that the Church create communities to be in charge; that people express themselves and fully participate; and that those communities discern the kind of ministry they engage in. It means collective ownership [*une prise en charge collective*]. Sister Alice advocated a renewed participation in which Christians could be engaged not only in sacramentalization and catechesis, but also in political and social life. She asked her audience not to lose sight of the mission of opening to the world. By virtue of this mission, new forms of ministry would emerge, like the diaconal couple and feminine ministry. She further asked her audience not to fear conflicts but allow believers to express their life experiences in order to grow in their faith and engagement.[74] She imagined building a pastoral ministry based on participation and sisterhood and brotherhood (fraternity), in which each member has a service to offer – a function. Alice Trudeau led a transformative force that implied the construction of a social imaginary that went beyond the boundaries of the congregation. A force building resistance started to play in the field.

Trudeau tried to reconstitute the congregation's intentionality within the framework of her vision, which embraced the Church and Catholic spirituality at large. Her vision was prophetic. The goals of her work were the restoration of persons in all phases of growth within the contours of the modern individual, but also within the contours of Ignatian spirituality, as well as communal integration.

In 1983, the same year that she made the presentation to the Congress of the Oblate Fathers, Alice Trudeau led the sisters in articulating a mission statement for the congregation, having as points of reference – illocutionary forces – "the needs of the suffering world"; the need to follow in the footsteps of the compassionate Jesus; and the need to be in solidarity with the promoters of peace, justice, and unity, empowered by faith and audacity. She defined the mission and vocation of the sisters as missionary-educators who enable individuals and groups, especially those who are deprived, to undertake their personal growth and self-actualization in order to build a more compassionate society and change the world.[75]

Figure 2.6 Painting by Sister Ghislaine Boucher. By this time (1980) paintings displayed in the convent, such as this still life by Sister Ghislaine Boucher, MO, were no longer strictly religious in their iconography. However, since the Renaissance, still life paintings have often been loaded with hidden religious meanings. This work follows this tradition with a couched criticism of the Church. The artist intended to convey a theme of transparency by depicting a glass pitcher and a glass bowl filled with water, to contrast with the opaqueness of the Church in the past. (Caption by Ana Jofré. See Bruno-Jofré and Jofré, "Reading the Lived Experience of Vatican II.") Reproduced with permission from Sister Cécile Fortier, General Superior for the Missionary Oblate Sisters.

In her Circular Letter 16 of 1985, "Onward in Hope," after re-election for a second term, Trudeau further articulates her vision for the Oblate community. She calls the sisters to have the courage to continue to discern together how God is calling them to build the future; the courage to be challengers – challengers can be disturbing – in their own local communities; the courage to perform concrete actions which are congruent with the radicalness of the Oblate mission statement; the courage to row against a certain current of resistance – of opposition, of apathy, of defeatism; the courage to overcome the obstacles, to untie the knots; the courage to forsake comforts in order to become a "prophetic leadership"; the courage to be audacious; the courage to lay aside personal preferences, to journey together; the courage to rally together and own the decisions of the Chapter; and the courage and loyalty to go to the persons concerned and have a discussion with them, rather than resisting and opposing them.[76] "Courage" was in this letter the key word in her attempt to rally the sisters.

The letter talks of her great hopes for the congregation and characterizes the participants in the Chapter as "multipliers," as proclaimers of Good News – those who, like John the Baptist, will prepare and pave the way so that the animation of the capitulary documents will be empowered by a dynamic thrust and a strength.

In this letter, she wrote,

> What are we doing in the face of this suffering world? Do we allow ourselves to be evangelized? Our society needs Oblates who are informed, authentic, and convinced.
>
> We feel within ourselves the need to be recognized for who we are. And, it follows that our contact with others must operate from person to person. In a broken, isolated world – prostitutes, divorcees, homosexuals, prisoners, refugees, rejectees – all thirst for acceptance, all need to find meaning to their life, a well-filled life.[77]

The letter tries to motivate new initiatives, new ministries – but not apart from the congregation – and urges the sisters "not to be afraid" and to act in ways that are creative and liberating. "With Jesus, the liberator par excellence, we will walk with a new vision of the future. We will be able to be Women of Good News, creators of unity, at the fore-front to detect what is most needed in the world, and thus, radiate life."[78]

The letter also includes small concrete and large potential initiatives that could involve the entire community. It advocates a closer relationship with teachers, offering courses in the schools where the Oblates still have a presence, personal and community renewal, planning, and collaboration.

Trudeau strongly believed in the full engagement of lay people in the apostolate. Indeed, Sister Rose Marie Viallet recalled that when Trudeau became principal of the elementary school in Assiniboia (she was assigned there from 1966 to 1973), she involved lay people. Mixing with lay people was something new – as Sister Viallet said, it was a new way of doing things. Interestingly, some sisters resented that Trudeau could consider lay people more important than themselves; however, as Viallet made clear, Trudeau was capable of devoting attention both to lay people and, as superior of the house, to each sister in particular.[79] In the Circular Letter under discussion, Trudeau stresses the need for promoting a responsible and committed laity and the relevance of offering the Spiritual Exercises in Daily Life. She states that she wants to open wide the Advisory Committee to lay people, and the sessions of the next Chapter to the Associates, and also to involve young adults in the congregation's work. It is important to note the tensions in Trudeau's vision between the radicalness of the commitment she is pursuing and the unclear relation with the Church's control that is mentioned in various places in the letter. For example, the letter states, "We will be able to allow the breath of life which animates us, to transform society and make it more Gospel-oriented."[80] Yet, it also says, "In hope, we will build the Congregation of today and of tomorrow, remembering the dream Mgr Langevin had in wanting his Oblates to be 'Daughters of the Church' in the fullest sense of the word, that is, at the service of the needs of the times in which we are living."[81]

In order to understand the tensions mentioned and the underlying intentionality, that is, the illocutionary force coordinating the meanings of the various statements, it is important to read the letter in relation to both the mission statement and also, in particular, the presentation to the Oblate Fathers. Trudeau sought a profound transformation of her community that could not take place without a parallel transformation of the Church. However, she seemed to think at the time that immediate contextual changes – for example, a transformation of the way the clergy, with whom the Oblates Sisters related, and the Oblate Fathers did things, as she proposed in her presentation to the Oblate Fathers – could make a difference. This new way of understanding the Church would demand a different social imaginary and new relations of power, and, as she said, a new mentality. Trudeau tried to work things out within the boundaries of her own context. She aimed at enacting her vision of more egalitarian and collaborative structures for ministry, and a democratic opening with strong participation of lay people living the priesthood of the baptized. In a way, she was enacting her own reading of Vatican II that, for example, had called for spiritual formation and leadership among the laity, a call supported by the Canadian bishops.[82]

Trudeau did not see the complexity of the institutional Church and the difficulties associated with relinquishing privileges. She was motivated by the possibility of substantial changes, but Vatican II had not expected congregations of religious to go as far. Those resisting her vision did not leave materials regarding their differences for the archives, but during her second term, the balance of forces started to incline toward those aiming at controlled changes within Church structures and directives without major challenges to dominant powers. By dealing with concrete situations affecting what she considered the dignity and self-worth of the sisters, Trudeau went as far as she could during her tenure as superior general.

For example, during her second and third years, Sister Trudeau had her first struggle with the bishops when she decided that the sisters working in pastoral ministry should have a signed contract with the local priest or bishop. She was motivated by the realization of how little a reward the sisters received for their work and that they did not have even a day off, while the priests did. With help from the Canadian Religious Conference, by the end of her second term in 1989, every sister in parish ministry had a contract. As Trudeau said, it was important that each sister be able to say "Yes, I do have recognition. Though I've left teaching, it is not a diminished ministry that I have."[83]

Significantly, Trudeau was concerned with the situation of the Aboriginal peoples even before John Paul II's 1984 address to the "Amerindians" during his visit to Canada.[84] The pope's address inspired the 1985 Chapter to write a document called "Pastoral Work with the Amerindians."[85] What the document reveals can be attributed to either lack of understanding, or to negotiations with opposing approaches, since at the time, the congregation was already becoming a field with two positions regarding renewal. On one side, the document gives thanks to the sisters who served in the (later denounced) residential and day schools of Manitoba, Saskatchewan, Ontario, and Alberta, hence revealing support for the residential schools. On the other side, there are signs of awareness of the struggle of the Aboriginal peoples and an expression of solidarity. The document says that the congregation could not ignore the fact that "our Indian brothers for more than ten years now have been claiming their civil and social rights. They wish to control their future, to preserve their cultural characteristics, to set up a school system that will respect their languages. Moreover, we note the fact that in many places the native people are among the poorest and the most marginalized of our society."[86] Referring to John Paul II's address, the document states that the Aboriginal peoples ("Indians," in the language of the document) suffered from "our slowness in rightly understanding their identity and their aptitudes to participate in directing their own future."[87] To underscore that point, it states that the sisters felt that they were called to offer their solicitude, as well as their compassion for their suffering, and to help them to eliminate the cause of their distress.

Unresolved tensions appeared at other points in the "Pastoral" as well. The Missionary Oblate, it states, tries to grasp and appreciate the true values of the "Indian culture." That is followed by "These values are purified and ennobled by the Revelation of Jesus-Christ." The explanatory statement contains elements displayed also in Trudeau's thinking, as well as that of other forward-looking sisters:

> By his Gospel, Christ confirms the native peoples in their faith in God, in their attention to his presence, particularly in the heart of the elements of creation, in their dependence upon it, in their desire to worship him, in their gratitude for the gift of Mother Earth, in their concern for our planet, in the reverence with which they surround all of creation, and finally in their great respect for their elders. The world is in need that these values – and many others which the Amerindians possess – be perpetuated among them and be incarnated in our whole Canadian population. The Missionary Oblate, aware of her own poverty, opens wide her heart to receive the riches that are present in the culture and in the very soul of the native people among whom she works.[88]

To stress again, Sister Alice Trudeau was not understood by many; she had to deal with internal polarization between those who were engaged with her transformative vision and those who resisted, holding onto the capital of the past; the interplay of forces became somewhat structured. Even the congregation's reception of Vatican II was quite uneven. Sister Bernadette Boulet recalled, "I ask myself whether the Sisters understood what Vatican II wanted to achieve. Vatican II [documents] were not studied by many. There was a lot of immaturity. Alice suffered a lot because of that. This is why certain Sisters have not forgiven Alice yet."[89] Sister Marie Anne Fillion described Trudeau as a "clairvoyante"; "she could fully use her talents and could see what was needed, she saw the future."[90] Tétreault said that Trudeau dove into ideas and situations, she went deep into the problems and found the roots, and from there she reconstituted, rebuilt anew – that she had a sense of radicality.[91] The sisters remember the spiritual renewal with Trudeau, a process initiated by Sister Lea Boutin, that took new dimensions: St Ignatius Spiritual Exercises in Daily Life; Christian meditation after her formation with Father John Main, OSB, at a Benedictine Monastery in

Montreal; a holistic vision of spirituality; and embracing the embodiment of spirituality.

By 1989, at the end of her mandate, in light of persistent resistance, Sister Alice Trudeau subdued her tone. The way power relations worked did not favour her positioning. Only one year before ending her second term, Trudeau had appealed to the sisters to become "innovators" in the sense, she said, John Baptist Metz uses the term – that is, as "effective models" for the Church. She had reinforced her appeal by citing "Mutual Relations," published in 1978 by the Sacred Congregation for Religious and Secular Institutes, which emphasized the innovative role of the religious. She had also quoted an article from the congregation's new constitutions (1983) that read, "[we] are sent by Christ ... to cooperate with the Spirit who is continually recreating the world."[92] Yet Trudeau continued to insist that an innovative role could be accomplished through the congregation's exercise of a prophetic leadership carrying out a radical evangelization incarnated in the Oblate values. But for this kind of evangelization to take place, she said, it would be important to have the wisdom to make decisions that would be crucial to the values the congregation wanted to instill, and the goals it aimed to achieve. The problem was that the goals she had in mind were part of a configuration within the field that was embraced by only a sector of the congregation. Trudeau wanted the sisters to display creative energy and will to act in order to achieve the goals of the congregation. She badly wanted a successor who could pursue her vision. She borrowed from Walter Brueggemann's *The Prophetic Imagination*[93] a conception of the task of a prophetic leader – expressing a future full of hope, bringing those hopes to the public, speaking about real newness, and speaking the language of amazement.[94] As I wrote in *The Spiritual Journey of Alice Trudeau*, the main issue that afflicted her leadership remained her preoccupation with the future: "the collective inspiration to lead the community to the point of a united vision for change."[95]

The language of hope was no longer dominant, however, in Sister Trudeau's report as outgoing superior. It conveyed a new conceptual configuration. It reflected, by and large subtextually, the dominant position within the congregational field of an arrangement of ideas and social forces in which residual elements, described earlier as attachment to what were perceived as sources of respect and authority, conformity with the notion of working within the boundaries of the institutional Church, and fear, coexisted with the notions of transformative change. However, to repeat, this configuration of the transformative ideas – initiated by

Sister Lea Boutin, and developed in a new direction with a radical prophetic quality with Sister Alice Trudeau – was not accepted by many.

In her report, Trudeau acknowledged that during the congregations' Cycle of Life sessions of 1987–88, the community confronted the process of mourning and became aware of feelings of insecurity, pain, and suffering. Trudeau did an optimistic reading of the situation. "We have lived a collective mourning that allowed us to say farewell to the past."[96] This, she said, helped them liberate themselves and find new energies to confront the future. Hence her restatement of vision now contained a reference to suffering, to the cross. She also wrote that in view of the state of the congregation, the revitalization would be carried on by each person who had in her heart a vital regenerating force and that this did not happen without suffering, without the cross: "We must pay the price."[97] In her last call to the congregation Trudeau said, "In each age of the history of the Church, where there is a crisis, the Spirit of God raises saints. These persons are always at the origin of a very profound renewal. Today we must pray with perseverance that God calls forth prophets and holy men and women. Thus we can hope for a new beginning for the congregation."[98]

Trudeau's reading of Vatican II was mediated by her surrounding reality; it was less grounded in intellectual readings – but they were not absent – than in her radical sense of dealing with injustice and suffering. She began from a profound feeling of other people's pain and the need for healing. But her congregation developed into a divided field. Many felt more comfortable with changing only the language of the congregation, rather than actually challenging residual parameters or the visible and invisible power boundaries of the Church. The dominance of plurality in the modern world, in which Christianity had become just one of the many worldviews and value systems in Western societies, became a challenge, as Berger puts it, for religion.[99] I would add that this plurality was intertwined with strong secularization processes in society at large.

Trudeau did not fully consider the contradictions emerging from the Vatican itself, or the conservative reaction, or the contradictions arising from the adaptation of the Church to the Western world without questioning its socio-economic foundations. As happened with radical Christians in Latin America, Sister Alice did not assess her real possibilities within the Church, and the working of power at various levels of the institution. To complicate matters, neither the council documents nor the conditions of reception in the congregation as well as in the Church had left space for a renewal based on a prophetic call, a critique of patriarchy, and a deep commitment to social justice. The reading of Medellín (1968) and its liberating utopia and the familiarity with feminist theology did not help to obliterate residual elements in the congregation and to "recreate in hope" the vision and mission of a congregation at a time when congregations were decreasing in membership.[100] The congregation could not create a new social imaginary or articulate a challenging, living, collective intentionality. The lack of new sisters only added to this conjuncture. By the early 1990s, there were no recruits. Central tenets of Trudeau's vision were continued by Tétreault and other sisters in interaction with the new leadership and within the parameters of an aging membership.

Early in the 1990s, Sister Alice resignified her commitment in a personal way in reference to oppression, power relations, and social transformation.[101] They went beyond the institutional boundaries of her congregation and of the Church itself.

BREAKING WITH THE BOUNDARIES

When Sister Alice Trudeau ended her second term as superior general in 1989, she had tested the limits of her own resources, of her community, and of the Church as an institution. Trudeau and Fortier (current superior of the Missionary Oblate Sisters) began a three-year formation program at the Institut de Formation Humaine Intégrale de Montréal (IFHIM, Institute of Integral Human Formation). Sister Alice needed a means for individual and social transformation. Earlier in her life she had discovered that the Personality and Human Relations workshops designed by André Rochais, who was influenced by humanist psychologist Carl Rogers, gave her means to pursue her growth ("there is within me more than me"), to cultivate openness to relationship ("the personal relation is not opposed to the communal"), and to exercise freedom by being true to her own conscience. However, despite sharing with Rochais the trust in the value and innate goodness of each person, Trudeau found that PHR did not help her to support the person in her lived experience to move toward transformation.

Dr Jeannine Guindon founded the institute (IFHIM) in cooperation with Sister Marie-Marcelle Desmarais, Congregation of Notre Dame (CND). Its goal was to lead the individual to become conscious of her vital human strengths and to help her realize how they could be actualized in

Lord Jesus
Help us to become
fully alive, fully human.
Create within us
strong desires for compassion,
gentleness and forgiveness.
Call us to be like yourself
wounded healers, gentle healers.
Teach us to speak
when it is time,
To listen
when it is time,
To be fully present
when it is time.
Give us a single heart,
a discerning heart, a loving heart.
Teach us to weep,
to laugh, to pain,
To be with one another
in our sorrows and in our joys.
Jesus, may we always give others
the space they need to grow
To bloom, to blossom,
to emerge, to be themselves.
by Alice Trudeau, m.o.

Figure 2.7 A prayer by Alice Trudeau. Created from the original by Angela and Rob Pietrobon. Reproduced with permission from Sister Cécile Fortier, General Superior for the Missionary Oblate Sisters.

spite of traumatic lived experiences. According to the program at IFHIM, a concept of energy that is either mobile (energy that fluctuates, moves in every direction), autonomous (energy that is channelled, harnessed), or bound (energy that is blocked, trapped) is central to the process of actualization of human strengths. The harnessing of this energy could lead to bodily, psychological, and spiritual autonomy.[102] The process of actualization was the integration of the unconscious and the conscious, the cognitive and the affective. Becoming conscious of something required a re-reading of lived experiences; the re-appropriation was achieved when the person was able to interiorize, keep, and integrate what was lived in her own human vital strengths.[103]

In December 1991, the coordinating team of the Oblate Sisters' Renewal Centre, made up of Sisters Dora Tétreault, Lea Boutin, Cécile Fortier, and Alice Trudeau, met with Sister Marie-Marcelle Desmarais in Montreal in an attempt to discern a collective project of integral growth for the Missionary Oblate Sisters, having as its starting point social commitment, and social and personal transformation. The mission of the project was defined as follows: "We want to be at the fore-front in order to be a bridge between leaders and the minorities through growth and dialogue/joint action for justice and social transformation."[104] The project did not prosper, however.

Trudeau and Fortier graduated from IFHIM in 1992. During 1993 and 1994, they offered sessions of holistic human development in the formation of laypersons for the ministry, through the Nathanaël Programme, and individual accompaniment, at the Missionary Oblate Aulneau Renewal Centre. At that point the centre had begun to offer professional counselling services, especially for low-income families.

Trudeau and Fortier both had training and experience in Ignatian Spiritual Exercises, and they found a relationship between the spiritual exercises and the IFHIM approach of the vital human strengths. In 1993, in a presentation she made at the Jesuit Congress of Ignatian Spirituality, Trudeau stated that both visions – Ignatian Spiritual Exercises and the Actualization of Vital Human Strengths – were grounded in a dynamic vision of the person, the human and spiritual growth of the person being their common goal. Both, she said, pay more attention to being with the person and accompanying her in her path, step by step, in a process of integration, than to the content of that person's experience. The same principles applied to becoming the agent of one's own human and spiritual growth. Love of one's self was essential to recognizing and loving others and for being present in God, for learning to love God.[105] In an interview conducted by Trudeau, Hélène Kilimnik, psychologist with IFHIM, stated that the Spiritual Exercises seek a movement of spiritual growth at the level of faith based on Scripture and Christian spirituality, and that the approach of the vital human strengths (AFVH) seeks a movement of human growth based on psychology.[106]

On 4 August 1994, Sister Alice received a call from the director of IFHIM to respond to the need for the reconstruction of persons traumatized by ethnic wars in Rwanda. She went through a process of discernment. In her written personal reflections, she registered: "Different Stances – Saying No – Road being closed, blocked; energy blocked – Saying Yes – Opening up to new challenges. What can I bring? My skills, tools, expertise, resources. Opening up to building bridges – Manitoba – Rwanda."

Sister Alice decided to go and gave her official answer to IFHIM on 5 September 1994.[107] Before she left (on 13 January 1995) to fulfill her mission with the Rwandan refugees in Goma, Democratic Republic of the Congo (at the time, Zaïre), I spoke with her.[108] Her pain for what could not be, and her realization of the resistance to her vision was evident.

> Even if I were to stay, like staying here, my ministry here I love it, because I know I work with leaders and there is an impact … But in terms of the Community, I don't sense they are losing a leader. I sense even that my going away, my leaving helps. And I am not saying this out of resentment but I think it is part of reality, and the reality being that my vision is a threat. Even my going to Rwanda, I didn't see this at first, but a good friend of mine said: "What is this silence all about?" There is a reason for the silence, of not speaking about my going away and about the project. Like saying: "It is not a Community project because I have been asked by the Institute [in Montreal]." And I think that is the tension that we are going through and that is part of the reality.
>
> And therefore, let's say for myself this new project is like a second wind for me … I don't know how long I will last, that is if my health gives in. I do not know that. It is an unknown. But what I know is maybe that is where I can best bring my contribution.[109]

Fortier wrote the following words in her farewell to Sister Alice, her close friend and partner in work, before Trudeau left for Africa in early 1995: "You are leaving with the most precious tool, the most powerful, that of love. It is your capacity for love that does not cease to fill me with wonder, to call me forth and inspire me. God is so clearly present and active in your choices to open up. This is what I want to celebrate

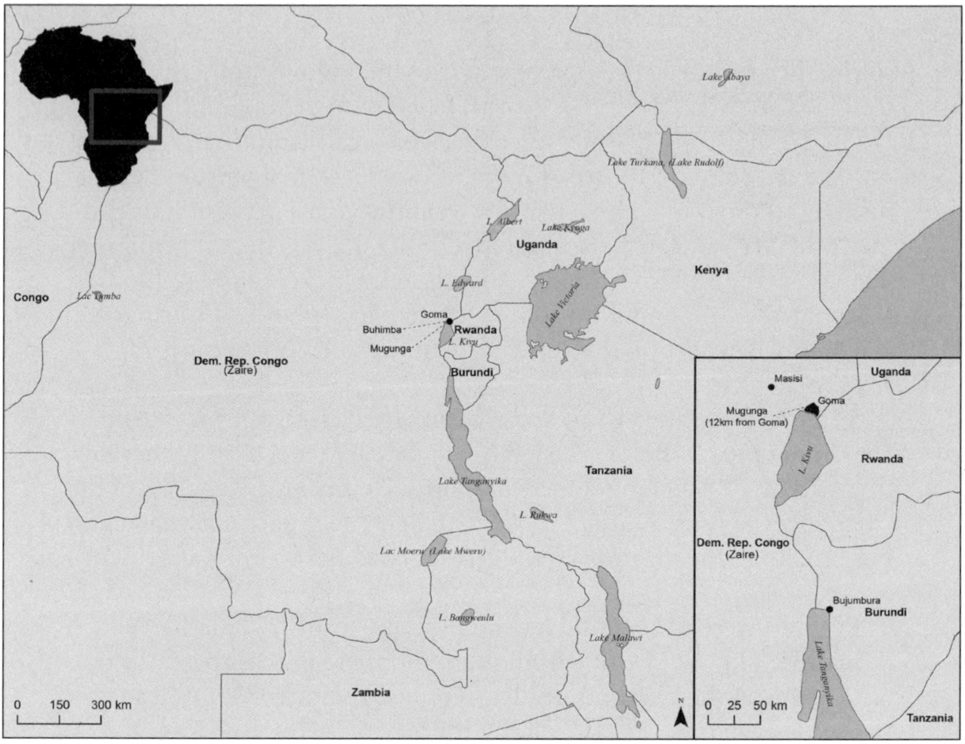

Figure 2.8 Map of Central Africa. Map designed by Graham Pope.

with you as I say 'Good-bye.' I keep you in my heart with love and in the strength that energizes you. My prayer is with you, dear 'lil friend.'"[110]

On 1 August 1995, Fortier joined Alice in Goma.

Africa was not an unknown missionary land for the Oblate Sisters. The congregation had a mission in Béré, Chad, from 1971 until 1993, involving the creation of a community centre offering literacy courses, sewing, and health care, plus parish youth animation in collaboration with the Capuchin Fathers. The Oblate Sisters also had a mission in Moundou (Chad), where Sister Marguerite Boily established or reorganized Catholic schools. And in Cameroon, from 1986 to 1996, the sisters had worked in parish community building and promotion of women, and offered Bible and religious courses.[111] As well, the bishop of Bogo wanted to have a "thriving Christian presence" and to create small faith communities.[112]

The "mission" in Central Africa was different this time. It did not aim at teaching religion or representing the Catholic faith in a direct way. In July 1994, Sister Marie-Marcelle Desmarais, CND, director of IFHIM, had been asked to send an intervening team to the Buhimba refugee camp for non-accompanied children (*Enfants rwandais non accompagnés*)

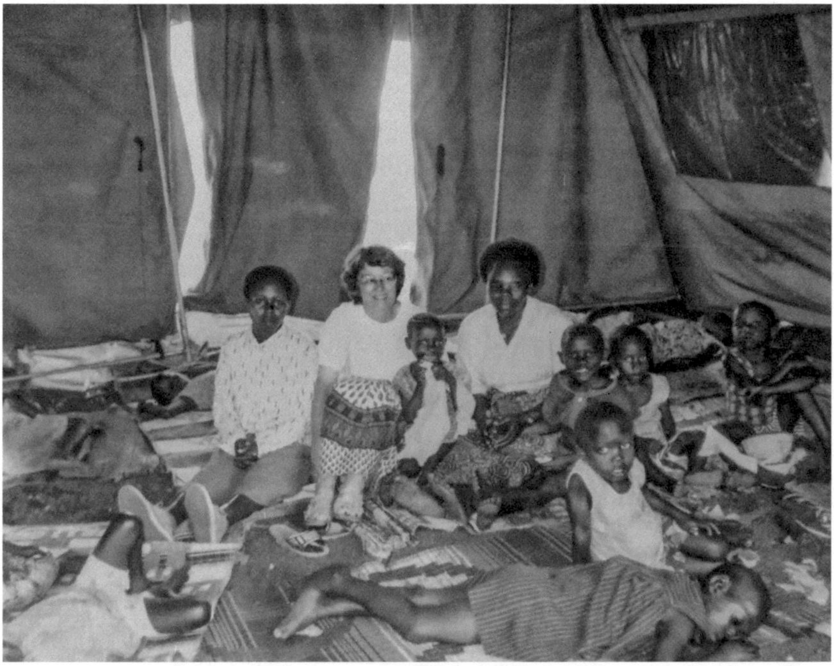

Figure 2.9 Sister Cécile Fortier with refugee children in a camp in Goma, DRC. The gaze of this group portrait is one of empathy, as she presents herself as part of this family, sitting at their level, in physical contact among them. Reproduced with permission from Sister Cécile Fortier, General Superior for the Missionary Oblate Sisters.

in Goma, Democratic Republic of the Congo. Desmarais sent three *formatrices*, Trudeau and Sisters Marie-Blanche LeBlanc and Lucette Dugas from the Religieuses Hospitalières de Saint-Joseph, followed by Fortier.[113] In the Buhimba Camp there were around 3,000 *enfants non accompagnés* (ENA).

From 8 February 1995 to the end of April 1996, the sisters were engaged in the intensive formation of fifty-two educators, camp leaders, organizers, and health workers, who could work with the ENA.[114] This was the Aid to the Reconstruction of Persons/Appui à la Reconstruction des Personnes (ARP) project. The project was financially supported by OXFAM Quebec (Oxford Committee for Famine Relief) and Terre Sans Frontières (Earth without Borders [TSF]), a non-profit support organization from Montreal, founded by a Frère de l'instruction chrétienne/Brother of Christian Instruction (FIC) in 1979.[115] By means of the process of actualization of vital human strengths, educators became equipped to deal with children who were traumatized by the psychological shock of what they had lived through. ARP sought to rebuild their confidence in themselves and in others; to re-establish pride and openness to the other as person in spite of differences; to regenerate the social fabric; and to learn to become artisans of peace.[116] Thus, an immediate task was to teach educators to actualize their own vital strengths and integrate their own traumas in order to help the children do the same.

When Fortier arrived in Goma in August 1995, a program of forced repatriation from the camp, which included ARP educators and organizers, had created a climate of insecurity and shaken ARP. Fortier and Trudeau became close to the children, with whom they built privileged relations.[117] However, the work at the Buhimba camp in Goma was discontinued in April 1996 after the government of Zaïre decided in March that only essential services could continue in the camp, and that non-essential services like education and commerce had to cease immediately.[118] The camps were disbanded. In any case, the situation was untenable since the deposed Rwandan political and military leaders had taken control of the camps, bringing with them their own economic resources (including Rwanda's hard currency), vehicles, and tons of coffee.[119] As Howard Adelman said, "[The] UNHCR [United Nations High Commissioner for Refugees] did little to prevent it; eventually, their rebuilding [the Rwandan military] was indirectly facilitated by UNHCR financial support. Many have questioned UNHCR's approach to the camps, as well as the attitudes of the non-governmental organizations that worked with them. They charge that UNHCR failed to provide security – that in concentrating on delivering needed food and medicine in the camps, it ignored the refugees' human rights."[120]

After a period of reflection between January and February 1996, the trainers, in conjunction with IFHIM, TSF, and OXFAM Quebec, decided to carry on a research action project in the Buhimba camp (ENA) and in the Mugunga camp (reunification Caritas-ENA).[121] The reports from that period contain interesting personal testimonies of trainers and people reached by the program, but there is very limited reference to the context. The letters compiled also show a climate of tension and danger, particularly during 1996.[122]

Trudeau and Fortier were ready to return to Canada in May 1996 when Congolese leaders from the area of Masisi sent a request to the director of Terre Sans Frontières for an Aid to the Reconstruction of Persons Program for the Congolese population in Goma.[123] From the start of the war, around 180,000 displaced people had moved to the poorest neighbourhood of the city of Goma.[124] The two Oblate Sisters worked

Figure 2.10 Sisters Cécile Fortier and Alice Trudeau on the road leading to a refugee camp in Goma, DRC. The photograph appears to have been taken candidly and seems to imply some level of integration into their new environment. The photograph speaks of two women out for a stroll on a beautiful day in a public space. Their demeanour is that of relaxed comfort, as if they were walking in their own neighbourhood; their contented expressions do not betray the foreignness of their surroundings. Reproduced with permission from Sister Cécile Fortier, General Superior for the Missionary Oblate Sisters.

there from May to October 1996, at which time, due to the upcoming civil war in Zaïre, they were evacuated and moved to Nairobi (Kenya) and returned to Canada in December 1996. They wrote:

> As members of the Security Committee of the High Commissariat of the United Nations for Refugees, we were taken in charge by the United Nations, who ensured our security in a vigilant manner to the end. We were evacuated with around twenty expatriates on Saturday, 26 October 1996, via an airplane from the International Red Cross. In spite of the tense climate in the city of Goma and the airport, the presence of our security agents allowed us to leave without problems. This has enabled us to remain calm and in peace, and live these events in solidarity with the people from Goma and the Rwanda refugees in the camps. Once we arrived at

Figure 2.11 Sister Alice Trudeau in Goma with Roger, chief of security. He accompanied her and the team to the sessions every day. They are at the formation house at Lake Kivu, Goma, Zaïre. This picture was taken in June 1995 and sent by Trudeau to Sister Dora Tétreault. Reproduced with permission from Sister Cécile Fortier, General Superior for the Missionary Oblate Sisters.

> Wilson airport in Nairobi, Kenya, we were welcomed by members of CIRC [International Red Cross] of Nairobi, who drove us to the Centre of the Mill Hill Missionaries. We spent a month in Nairobi working on our reports for our organizations and IFHIM.[125]

Some letters and telegrams written by Fortier and Trudeau when they were abroad are about lack of security and turmoil, but the sisters did not discuss what was going on politically. Often they reported the destruction of a village, requests for help from parish priests, or dangerous situations.[126] Despite that, it seems that the central focus remained the reconstruction of persons as a way out of the humanitarian crisis.

However, the reality was that together with genuine refugees, "there were perhaps a hundred thousand militant Hutu *génocidaires* and *iterahumwe* (those who attack together) who were responsible for the killings in Rwanda."[127] The militants in the camps were a threat to civilians; women were raped; refugees were robbed of their rations.[128] In a fax to Trudeau and Fortier, dated 17 October 1996, Sister Marie-Marcelle Desmarais shared a question that had been raised in relation to the work in Bukavu, although it would have been the same question, she said, for Goma.

> We were wondering whether the changes were real or whether it was just the perception of the animators that had changed as a result of their insertion. It would be interesting if local people could attest that there have been differences and if so, in what way? Were the groups interested in active non-violence or peace reached through one or the other of the multipliers? Through sessions? How would you describe, and not only successful results? All the facts gathered that will be published will report the successful ones. You have certainly observed failures, limitations, resistance, partial success, and other unresolved obstacles. If we could point them out, this would make the successes more credible, I believe. It would give more realism.[129]

Upon returning to Canada, Trudeau and her colleague Sister Marie-Blanche Leblanc, SHSJ were sent by IFHIM and Terre Sans Frontières to Haiti. They remained there from April to June 1997 to evaluate the effectiveness of a centre for human promotion through the process of actualization of vital human strengths, which had been in operation for ten years.[130]

From 13 August to 28 September 1997, Trudeau and Fortier conducted an action-research project in Goma in an environment of fragile security. The purpose of the project was to evaluate the impact of ARP and identify what had been retained by the participants, and revise the formation seminars in light of what people had experienced, and how.[131] The sisters noted that during the training there was an effort to help people differentiate between inner impressions and experience of reality – meaning, in this case, differentiating image from reality, moving to a more real representation of self, and, when referring to God, shifting from an image of God as caregiver to a personal God who invites them to become active participants in the caring of God for others. Following the sisters' reports, ARP began to include notions of opening up, loving versus refusing to love, and accompanying the person in her pain.

Figure 2.12 Sister Cécile Fortier in Bujumbura, Burundi. A small group session in Bujumbura. Sister Cécile Fortier is sitting with others in a circle. The only clue that marks her as a facilitator is that she is not taking notes. In all other respects, the people are visually positioned as equal adults. Reproduced with permission from Sister Cécile Fortier, General Superior for the Missionary Oblate Sisters.

Starting in September 1997, Trudeau and Fortier became engaged in a new intervention project similar to the first one in Goma, this time in Bujumbura, Burundi – also affected by a civil war – joining Sister Joséphine Pauline Ndabemeye, who had taken a two-year preparation course at IFHIM in Montreal.[132] The project lasted until June 2002. The team worked in different settings and interacted with many levels of society – street children, orphans due to war or AIDS, workers, widows, social workers, students. In 2002, a local team took over. During their time in Burundi, the sisters and their team often went to Goma, where they became established in September 2002 and provided support both to the population after the eruption of volcano Nyragongo and to the nucleus of ARP Goma. On 27 October 2004, Trudeau died of a stroke in Nairobi. Fortier returned to Canada. The work was handed over to the Congolese team.[133]

The mission carried out by Trudeau and Fortier in Central Africa was distinct. The sisters were among women and men religious belonging to different congregations and working with NGOs. Women and men

Figure 2.13 Sister Alice Trudeau in a community class. In this candid photograph, Sister Alice Trudeau is shown in the act of listening. She is visiting a group of Muslim women involved in a sewing project. She does not place herself at the front of the classroom as the sole teacher, but as part of a collaborative effort in which all are engaged. Reproduced with permission from Sister Cécile Fortier, General Superior for the Missionary Oblate Sisters.

religious working with NGOs was not unusual. But in this case, their mission had a non-denominational, even secular, tone. It was open to a pluralism that broke otherness. Its non-conversionist character and lack of religious markers is not surprising, given the historical conditions framing those projects. During the Rwandan genocide, between 6 April and mid-July 1994, one million people were killed by soldiers, militias, and ordinary civilians. The shocking point is that the history of Rwanda prior to and after independence, as Safari wrote, is connected to the influence of Christian churches, in particular the Catholic Church.[134] At the time of the genocide, Rwanda was 90 percent Christian, and 62 percent of the population was Catholic. The greatest number of killings took place in Rwanda's churches or on church premises. It is not only that clerics, religious people, and church personnel were targeted by the mobs, but that a number of clerics were involved in the killings themselves. As Safari, a priest himself, wrote, "some priests, religious brothers and nuns have been accused by victims of being active agents during the killings."[135]

Figure 2.14 Sister Alice Trudeau visiting a displaced Congolese family who had to flee their town because of war. The composition of this photograph places Trudeau as a secondary character. The two people standing appear to be posing for the photograph, while Alice concerns herself with the children on the floor. This is telling of how she perceives herself in her mission work. Reproduced with permission from Sister Cécile Fortier, General Superior for the Missionary Oblate Sisters.

The mission in Africa was in line with Trudeau's vision for her congregation, one that, as stated, was not fully shared by all the members. It was within the parameters of the broad statements about mission elaborated by the congregation after Vatican II; those statements encouraged the cultivation of individual sisters' personal interests and inclinations. This particular mission in Africa, carried out by Fortier and Trudeau, was not a community project. Before leaving, Trudeau had clearly conveyed the feeling that the mission she was embracing was seen as something belonging to her, not to the community,[136] although it was approved by the congregation and was included in the Chapters' reports.

The African mission was indeed within the reconstituted spirituality based on a new understanding of reparation grounded in the evangelical notion of poverty and a theology from human experience. It was in line with the shift made by the congregation from a language of mortification and grace to a language of social justice. The congregation rooted a vision of justice in the founder's (Archbishop Langevin) vision of justice for

Soeur Alice Trudeau

Missionnaire oblate du Sacré-Coeur et de Marie-Immaculée

Née le 28 mars 1935
Ile-des-Chênes, Manitoba

Décédée
le 27 octobre 2004
Nairobi, Kenya

Figure 2.15 Sister Alice Trudeau on a mototaxi. This was the Sisters' ordinary way of travelling in the city of Goma. This photograph was used to memorialize Alice. The portrait the sisters chose was a candid environmental one rather than a constructed studio portrait. She is on the back of a motorcycle, happily waving; the image expresses an adventurous, friendly, open, and trusting nature. Her hairstyle, decorative bag, and bright shirt are evident personal signifiers, ways in which she chose to individuate herself. (Thanks to Ana Jofré for her input.) Reproduced with permission from Sister Cécile Fortier, General Superior for the Missionary Oblate Sisters.

the Catholic people in Manitoba and for Franco-Manitoban Catholics. The mission undertaken by Trudeau and Fortier had approval from the congregation. However, it went beyond that. What did this apostolate mean in the spiritual life of Trudeau? In the rest of this section, I try to answer that question.

The apostolate in Congo and Burundi was in line not only with Trudeau's vision for her congregation, but also with her prophetic vision, her search to overcome the institutional boundaries to her Catholic spirituality, and her desire to reach out in an apostolate sustained by uncompromised love and social justice. She was able to connect her commitment to Ignatian spirituality with a sense of the body, the psychological formation from Rochais's workshops, as well as with IFHIM's aims at transforming individuals and generating a multiplying effect through trainers/multipliers immersed in its psychological/spiritual approaches.

The apostolate in Africa would take place in a field in which limits were initially set by the reality of the camps themselves, and so it was not the institutional constraints of the congregation or the Church, but the structural and bureaucratic constraints of international organizations and their reluctance to engage in operations, that made it difficult to prevent or deal with violence.[137] The constraints did not affect Trudeau's inner intentionality. Therefore, when the time came Trudeau and Fortier would work with the same communities, reconstructing their strengths and building projects of an imagined future with them.

What makes this particular mission even more unique is that its purpose was not to evangelize but to offer skills in order to take charge of one's life and to manage one's emotions, such as anger, hostility, and grief. The important thing was the person, no matter what ethnic background or faith; therefore, the formation sessions were offered to Catholics, Protestants, Muslims, and people with other belief systems. Fortier wrote that their goal was to train caregivers who would continue to minister to their people. The spirituality was revealed in the testimony. Fortier said that she and Trudeau were living the charism in a different context.

A long-term analysis reveals continuity between the prophetic vision of Alice Trudeau as superior and the two sisters' work in Central Africa. It was a vision that had been supported by important sectors of the congregation, including Fortier. The notion of transformation, of following in the footsteps of Jesus, and the definition of the prophetic leader as expressing a future full of hope (taken from Walter Brueggemann) are fully incarnated in Trudeau's mission in Africa, even as it exhibits some political naivete.

CONCLUSION

The Second Vatican Council and its resolutions opened a door for dealing with latent tensions, contradictions, and losses of meaning; it was an enabling force. In this chapter, a *longue durée* approach has been used in order to help grasp the magnitude of the crisis that followed Vatican II: the conjunctures, how new intentionalities developed and often became truncated, and the barriers to construing a community social imaginary (in Taylor's sense), and how the congregation was unable to redefine the expectations for the community as a collective and re-imagine themselves as such. (More recently the community has pulled together while confronting their end and cultivating their legacy.)

The Missionary Oblate Sisters of the Sacred Heart and Mary Immaculate went through a renewal process in the midst of reconstituting its relationship with the world and in the midst of theological renewal. The courses on theology, readings from Yves Congar and Karl Rahner to Betty Friedan, and in the 1970s and 1980s, from feminist theologians, along with new interactions with a plural world and a search for personal identity through Carl Rogers's psychological tenets (through André Rochais's workshops) created an invigorating context for the sisters. The congregation participated regularly in the Canadian Religious Conference (CRC) – analyzed in the first chapter of this book – and Trudeau was actually supported by the CRC in some of her confrontations with the clergy, as mentioned before.

The painting for the hundredth anniversary of the Missionary Oblate Sisters has a cosmic dimension, a new vision rooted in an ecological understanding of the world, and a view of the future: the lay people following Virgin Mary, the leader who inspired the foundation of the congregation, in a long procession. The lay people appear to be picking up the work of the mission. That utopian vision does not seem to correlate with the actual, difficult path characterizing the process of change and the resistance in the congregation. The sister who painted it tried to make sense of the congregation's past in light of an imagined future grounded in memories, what Paul Ricoeur refers to as a "space of experience," and of their expectations for the future (Ricoeur's "horizon of expectation"). However, in actuality, the community developed as a divided field with an intense interplay between residual elements from the past, institutional constraints, and visions of change. The congregation could not reach a common purpose as imagined in the painting.

The preoccupation with the autonomous self and the reconstitution of the self brought out in the congregation the tensions within modernity between autonomy and fragmentation. For a period of time, the congregation issued statements and resolutions choosing life over death, individual over group ministries, continuation of community projects, notions of a new way of being religious, but no new articulation of a common transformative vision and mission. When Trudeau moved from ambivalence toward a radical transformative position with a more defined path, the interplay between residual elements from the past, institutional constraints, and visions of change gave way in her second term to two well-defined positions in the field (which, to remind, I use to characterize the congregation). One was still attached to residual elements but wrapped in a new language and changes in daily life, as well as a somewhat timid recovery of women's experiences, but not organized action. Those supporting this position played within the rules of the institution. The other position, led by Trudeau, represented a radical proposal for change; it embodied a prophetic vision. These differences were part of different ways of relating to the context and reading of Vatican II.

The radical prophetic vision of Trudeau went beyond the walls of the convent to embrace a challenging vision of the relationship of the congregation with the clergy and the Church and of the relationship between women religious and men religious. The pillar components of her positioning in the field included service, not to the clergy but to the people of God, with emphasis on the role of lay people as baptized (in reference to "the priesthood of the baptized"); a strong notion of social justice nourished in her feminism; the needs of the suffering world as central tenet of her intended actions; a movement away from subordination to the clergy toward equality and co-responsibility and from an authoritarian pastoral agency to one based on partnership, including the creation of structures to produce communal decisions with the clergy (in particular the Oblate Fathers). Her diagnosis of the reluctance of sectors of the congregation to embrace her vision is that they lacked "courage," a key term for Trudeau. The congregation needed courage, in her view, to overcome fear and comfortable positions.

Trudeau had a holistic vision of spirituality. It was a spirituality grounded in women's experience, her questioning of the role of women in the patriarchal structure of the Church, and in her conviction of the relationship between faith and social justice. In Trudeau's understanding of spiritual and personal development, there is an eclectic convergence of the Rogerian approach and its concern for existential freedom and personal growth, with Ignatian spirituality and with Christian meditation.

Trudeau's vision failed to take root in the congregation at large. At the same time, the members of the congregation had to confront the process of aging in the absence of new sisters to replace them. After her tenure as superior general, Trudeau, with Fortier, enrolled in the program of the Institut de Formation Humaine Intégrale de Montréal that focused on making individuals aware of their human strengths and ways of actualizing them in spite of traumatic experiences. First Trudeau and then Fortier responded to the IFHIM invitation to work with persons traumatized by the genocide in Rwanda and displaced in camps.

Trudeau's and Fortier's work within IFHIM in projects financially supported by non-governmental organizations such OXFAM Quebec and Terre Sans Frontières was one of testimony, where the spiritual and the psychological dimension intertwine without any goal of conversion. Trudeau's work in Central Africa was in line with her vision, shared by a group of sisters in the congregation, including Fortier and Tétreault. Trudeau's vision was one of social transformation, of the need to follow the steps of Jesus, of commitment to justice, of horizontal relations, of a way of living the Gospel.

The work in Africa was free from the constraints generated by the persistence of residual elements in the congregation, rooted in their old ways of being religious, fear of change, heightened awareness of the parameters set by the Vatican, as well as of the implications of the emergence of the autonomous self and the decline of vocations. In Africa, sisters Alice Trudeau and Cécile Fortier encountered a different set of political and social obstacles that did not set spiritual parameters to their work in the world.

3

Living Religious Life on a Broad Canvas: Vatican II and Sister Mary Alban (Bernadette) Bouchard, CSJ

Elizabeth M. Smyth

On 21 November 2014, Pope Francis issued an apostolic letter in which he proclaimed a "Year of Consecrated Life." Writing to the members of the worldwide communities of men and women religious, he quoted the words of his predecessor, Pope Saint John Paul II, to indicate the year's purpose: "You have not only a glorious history to remember and to recount, but also a great history still to be accomplished! Look to the future, where the Spirit is sending you, in order to do even greater things."[1]

Pope Francis reminded his readers that 2014 was the fiftieth anniversary of the promulgation of two documents of the Second Vatican Council (Vatican II) that had a profound impact on the religious life: Decree on the Adaptation and Renewal of Religious Life (*Perfectae Caritatis*/Perfect Charity) and the Dogmatic Constitution on the Church (*Lumen Gentium*/Light to Nations). Their implementation had a significant impact on how men and women both conceptualized and lived their lives as vowed religious. In fact, in the minds of some authors, such as journalist Ann Carey, the author of *Sisters in Crisis: The Tragic Unraveling of Women's Religious Communities*,[2] Vatican II destroyed religious life as it had been.

This chapter explores the impact of Vatican II on a Canadian congregation of women religious[3] – the Sisters of St Joseph of Toronto. Methodologically, this chapter uses a biographical approach for its analysis of primary and secondary sources. Robert Lee Miller describes the biographical method as "the collection and analysis of an intensive account of a whole life or portion of a life. The account may be reinforced by semi-structured interviewing or personal documents. Rather than concentrating upon a 'snapshot' of an individual's present situation, the biographical approach emphasises the placement of the individual within a nexus of social connections."[4] Lois Banner, Alison Booth, Ken Plummer, and Brian Roberts are among the scholars who have encouraged this approach as a means to create a textured, more nuanced understanding of history.[5] Historian Margaret MacMillan argues for the power of such an approach in her 2015 Massey Lectures. She recalls the observation of the English historian Thomas Carlyle that "the decree of good biography – and indeed of much good history – is to understand the relationship between individuals and their societies."[6] MacMillan concludes: "While a single life cannot stand in for a whole era, it can illuminate it, and make us want, indeed oblige us, to know more."[7] Thus, this chapter focuses on the life and writings of Marie (Mary) Bernadette Bouchard – in religion, Sister Mary Alban – drawing primarily from materials found in the Archives of the Sisters of St Joseph of Toronto. Sister Mary Alban was a life-long writer and has left an extensive collection of personal papers to which I was given unrestricted access. Her fonds include both published and unpublished articles, personal correspondence, photographs, audio recordings, and journals. I was also given access to other congregational and administrative records of the periods before, during, and after her life in religion.

Using a biographical framework, this chapter places Sister Mary Alban at the centre of an analysis of the changes in society and religious life experienced by members of the Sisters of St Joseph of Toronto specifically, and of Canadian women religious generally, during the sixty-year period bounded by the years 1950 and 2010. This chapter argues that one cannot separate the congregational response to the changes mandated by the reforms of Vatican II from two other elements: the historical roots of the changes to religious life initiated during the 1950s and the impact of the monumental social changes of the 1960s.

Bernadette Bouchard entered the Sisters of St Joseph of Toronto as a sixteen-year-old graduate of the sisters' convent boarding school in the farming town of Rosetown, Saskatchewan, in 1949. As Sister Mary Alban, she began her career as a teaching sister and worked in the community's elementary, secondary, and post-secondary institutions. A gifted teacher and voluminous writer, she was a well-published poet and textbook author. Her response to the social upheavals of the 1960s brought her to peace activism and social justice leadership. She worked at the United Nations in New York City, undertook a thirty-day fast at the White House, and was arrested for engaging in civil disobedience against Lytton Systems, the manufacturer of the guidance systems for the cruise missile. At age fifty-eight, when many would be considering retirement, she began a new career as a missionary in the barrios of Haiti where she wrote primers in Haitian Creole and worked with women to establish micro businesses. She stayed in Haiti for twenty-four years, returning to the Toronto motherhouse for treatment of what would be terminal leukemia. She died on 10 September 2013 at age eighty-two. Just before her death, Pax Christi, the Canadian branch of the International Catholic Peace Movement, named her the inaugural Teacher of Peace.

This chapter develops in four sections. It begins by situating women religious – and the congregation that Sister Mary Alban entered, the Sisters of St Joseph of Toronto – in the history of Canada, as well as highlighting the current historiographical significance of vowed women within the Roman Catholic Church. The chapter then explores how religious life changed in the twentieth century, specifically in the 1950s and 1960s, before discussing the impact of these changes on Sister Mary Alban's formation and life as a religious. The third section examines religious life from Vatican II to the present through an analysis of how the reconceptualization of living out the vows and congregational charism are evident through Sister Mary Alban's career and writings. The chapter returns to Pope Francis's call for a year on consecrated life and a discussion of his first encyclical, issued on 24 May 2015, On the Care for Our Common Home (*Laudato Si'*), linking these documents to Sister Mary Alban's environmental activism. The chapter concludes by situating the life of Sister Mary Alban within the overarching themes of this book.

BERNADETTE BOUCHARD BECOMES SISTER MARY ALBAN: WOMEN RELIGIOUS IN CANADA, 1639–1950

With the advent of permanent settlement in New France, the Roman Catholic Church responded to the spiritual, social, educational, and health care needs of the colonists and the Indigenous peoples by recruiting two communities of women religious to provide such services. Thus, in 1639, members of the Order of St Ursula (Ursulines of Tours), a teaching order, and the Religious Hospitaliers of St Augustine (Hospitaliers of Dieppe) journeyed to New France. Over the next three centuries, more than 160 religious communities of Roman Catholic and Anglican nuns and sisters were established or made foundations in Canada.

Communities of women religious have played a significant but understudied role in the history of Canada. Until the latter decades of the twentieth century, congregational histories were internally generated and tended to have pious and somewhat hagiographic overtones. When individual women religious were studied, they tended to be characterized as "woman worthies" such as the seventeenth-century mystic and writer Marie de l'Incarnation, whose letters provide historians with many insights into life in New France, or the founders of religious communities, such as the Congregation de Notre Dame's Marguerite Bourgeoys and the Grey Nuns' Marguerite d'Youville. More recently, historians have begun to explore the intersections between and among women religious and the larger society, especially within Quebec. There remains much work to be done,[8] especially focusing on anglophone congregations.[9]

The Sisters of St Joseph arrived in Upper Canada some 200 years after the first women religious arrived in New France. They were invited by Armand-François-Marie de Charbonnel, the second bishop of Toronto, to care for orphans, the poor, and the elderly in his large and disadvantaged diocese. The Sisters of St Joseph were founded in the mid-seventeenth century in LePuy, France, initially as a lay association of pious women dedicated to undertaking charitable work. In 1851, four sisters arrived in the mission field of Toronto via their initial North American foundation in Carondelet, Missouri, and their subsequent foundation in Philadelphia. Led by Mother Delphine Fontbonne, the community initially administered an orphanage and ministered to the needs of the "sick poor." The community attracted the interest and admiration of bishops, laity, and the larger secular society. Soon, young women presented themselves as postulants, and the Sisters of St Joseph quickly

Figure 3.1 Bernadette Bouchard, 1947. From the scrapbook entitled "My Sacred History. Sister Mary Alban Bouchard," Mary Alban Bouchard, CSJ, Personal Collection, CSJT Archives.

grew in numbers and expanded their geographic scope. The Toronto motherhouse would soon claim daughter congregations in five other dioceses: the Sisters of St Joseph of Hamilton, London, Peterborough, Sault Ste Marie, and Pembroke. Over the next 150 years, these six congregations established across Canada an array of educational, social, and health care institutions including elementary and secondary schools, convent academies and boarding schools, hospitals and schools of nursing, a university-based college, orphanages, homes for the aged, and houses of social service.

Like all religious congregations, the Sisters of St Joseph counted on a trinity of institutions – the Church, the school, and the family – to ensure that young women would heed the call of God to replenish their ranks. For a young French-Canadian girl growing up in rural Canada in the 1940s, it was the combination of these three that brought her to the Sisters of St Joseph.

Bernadette Marie Bouchard was born in Kerrobert, Saskatchewan, on 12 October 1931. She was the youngest of eight children of Leopold Bouchard and Adelia Poulin. In her two manuscript autobiographies, *Pieces of My Life: Selected Memoirs* and *West of the Third Meridian*, she described a family life in which faith played a central role. She recalled the family gathering for daily recitation of the rosary and described the challenges of travelling through the deep snow to attend Sunday mass.

Typical of a prairie childhood, Bernadette attended a one-room, non-denominational school. She received her religious formation and catechetical instruction at home. She remembered the first time she heard about sisters, and how the lifestyle captured her imagination. Again, as was a feature of life on the prairies – and indeed, of rural life in other provinces – women religious, who were full-time teachers in villages, towns, and city schools during the school year, were often missioned to teach catechism in rural areas during the school vacations. Bernadette recalled:

> When I was very young, perhaps five or six, I heard the priest announce on Sunday, "The Sisters are coming. There will be catechism for two weeks for the children." This created a considerable buzz of excitement in the church. I was puzzled because I did not know what was meant by "the Sisters." I had never seen "a Sister." After Mass I asked my mother who was coming? Who were "the Sisters"? She tried to explain in language I could comprehend that the Sisters were women who loved God very much, lived and worked and prayed together and did everything for God – like teaching little children and looking after sick people. I decided then that was a good and noble way to live one's life. I stowed this thought away in my heart and mind, like a seed planted deep in soil.[10]

After completing her elementary education, Bernadette pursued the first years of high school in her one-room school by correspondence and then enrolled in the boarding school of the Sisters of St Joseph in Rosetown, Saskatchewan. By that time, she considered herself an established poet and published author. She wrote, "I started at a very early age to write poetry to soothe my soul and be uplifted with the beauty of it. I remember one poem called 'Clouds' and another called 'Flowers' that were published in the *Western Producer* Pathfinders Page. The excitement of it! (But I wasn't lauded. We were a modest family!) The happiness was within and became a disease I could never throw, a habit I could never kick, to this day."[11]

Her experience in a convent boarding school exposed her to a daily routine that mirrored convent life, with studies and prayer interspersed. Bernadette found the experience both comforting and engaging, and reflected that life within a religious community would enable her to live her faith and employ her love of writing, "So before my graduation, I consulted with my parents and then made my application to enter the

Sisters of St Joseph of Toronto. At the age of sixteen, I set out to leave family, friends and career, and everything else, without regret but with gratitude, anticipation and a joyful heart. Obviously, I had not much of a 'career' to leave except that of a budding writer with a scholarship to the University of Saskatchewan which I thought was access to the world of literature I so loved. But now those pieces I had already had published I burned in the desire to leave everything behind. Ah, the ardor of youth! It is good to remember."[12]

The life that Bernadette had chosen was legally and spiritually regulated, governed by the 1935 *Constitutions of the Sisters of St Joseph of Toronto*. The *Constitutions* laid out with precision numerous elements of a sister's life. They required the congregation's members to live the vows of poverty, chastity, and obedience and to gain personal salvation through the service of neighbour by engaging in "the instruction and Christian education of the young and directions of works of charity such as orphanages, hospitals and homes for the poor and aged."[13] The *Constitutions* clearly stated the nature of the works to which the sisters would dedicate themselves, and to do otherwise was not permitted: "it is forbidden without permission of the Holy See to modify … or to add to it in a permanent and general way any works which are not comprised to this end."[14] Likewise, the *Constitutions* dictated the criteria for membership: "To be admitted into the Congregation, candidates must belong to a respectable family, be of good reputation, docile disposition, good judgment and have health sufficient to discharge the duties of the Congregation."[15]

After obtaining the requisite "certificates of Baptism and Confirmation, also a testimonial of good conduct signed by their parish priest or a well known ecclesiastic, and a certificate of health from a reliable doctor,"[16] a candidate presented herself as a postulant and would spend six months assessing the community and being assessed by it. If both she and the leadership of the congregation agreed, the postulant would become a novice. Thus, as hundreds of women had done before her, Bernadette Bouchard relinquished her name and her secular dress, and as Sister Mary Alban donned the habit of the Sisters of St Joseph on the Feast of St Joseph, 18 March 1949.

As a newly habited sister, Sister Mary Alban became a student, spending what is known as a canonical year in which she learned the foundations of her religious life: through studies of the *Constitutions* and *Book of Customs*. These documents set out the daily operations of the congregation, its historical and spiritual origins, its governance and cultural and operational features, and mandated specific spiritual practices. At the end of that year, the superior general told her that she would become a teacher and sent her to the Toronto Normal School to obtain certification as an elementary teacher. The *Constitutions* specified those qualities a teaching sister should display: "By word and example, the teachers should endeavour to inspire their pupils with a love of virtue; they shall strive to form their character, show them wherein true virtue consists and train them in the exercise of solid virtue."[17]

Teaching sisters were instructed to be "prudent, gentle and firm" with their pupils, "being careful to repress in themselves every inclination to impatience."[18] Under the vow of obedience, teaching sisters were instructed to focus on the study of religion and to prepare only those courses and classes to which they had been assigned: "The study and preparation of lessons, particularly the preparation of the Catechism lesson, shall be considered an important duty and teachers ought to use all the time that is allowed them; however they shall not apply themselves to any new study without the permission of the Directress of Schools."[19]

Sister Mary Alban taught in a number of elementary schools in Barrie and Toronto, succumbing on several occasions to the waves of childhood illnesses that often attacked a beginning teacher. When – and if – she had the time to reflect, she may have observed that even as she entered it, religious life was in the throes of change.

LIVING CHANGE IN RELIGIOUS LIFE

During the late 1940s and early 1950s, leaders of religious congregations and the Vatican began to look critically at how congregations of women religious were responding to the needs of the times. In 1949, for example, Sister Madeleva Wolff – a member of the Holy Cross Sisters and president of St Mary's College in South Bend, Indiana (the sister college to the Holy Cross Fathers' Notre Dame University) – presented her iconic work *The Education of Sister Lucy* in which she reflected on how sisters should be prepared for careers as teachers, stressing the need for post-secondary education and well-grounded pedagogical instruction. The following year, on 21 November 1950, Pope Pius XII issued *Sponsa Christi* (Spouse of Christ) – a document that reflected on papal enclosure.[20] He also convened the First General Congress of the States of Perfection, calling the superiors general of religious congregations to a meeting in Rome and thereby initiating discussions of modifying outmoded religious habits to make them more suitable to the modern world. As a result of these deliberations, the Vatican also called for changes in governance. One key element was eliminating hierarchical structures and empowering lay sisters (members of religious congregations who were responsible for the domestic labour needed to support the professional work of the choir sisters, who served as the professional class of teachers, nurses, social service workers, and administrators) by giving them a voice in the congregational governance meetings known as chapters. A second change was modification to religious habits, including redesigning veils and face pieces to make them more suitable for women who were now driving cars and operating machinery. As well, the heavy starching that was documented as a cause of inflammations and ear infections was eliminated. Bishop (and soon to be Cardinal) Louis-Joseph Suenens, Louvain University academic administrator, held discussions with women religious and secular and religious priests on the theology of a "nun's" vocation and debated how religious life should adapt to the times as he prepared his monograph, *The Nun in the Modern World*, which would appear in 1962.

As was the case with many other religious communities, the 1950s saw the Sisters of St Joseph of Toronto engaged with their local, national, and international colleagues. In 1950, the congregation celebrated the 300th anniversary of its founding by initiating discussions among the thirty-two independent branches of the North American Sisters of St Joseph that traced their roots back to LePuy-Lyon. Along with plays written to celebrate the occasion and pageants staged in the sisters' schools and colleges, the Sisters of St Joseph of Toronto collaborated with several of their sister congregations in the United States to translate and publish in English a collection of essays that analyzed the foundation of the congregation.[21] The sisters were already undertaking a systematic process of tracing their roots.

Sister Mary Alban participated in these celebrations. She attended and performed in historical plays written by her sister colleagues. She read the congregational history published in 1951 by Sister Mary Agnes Murphy, University of St Michael's College professor of French and the first woman to graduate with a degree from St Michael's. This history capitalized on Sister Mary Agnes's studies at the University of Grenoble and her visits to congregational birthplaces of LePuy and Lyon in the years just prior to the Second World War. Sister Mary Alban may have viewed Sister Mary Agnes as a model – for unlike nuns and sisters of previous generations, she was a writer who published under her own name. Even outwardly, the habit that Mary Alban wore had been modified from that worn by her predecessors. The late 1950s habit had far less fabric in the sleeves and the veil.

Sister Mary Alban's early life in religion had also been shaped by the fact that the Sisters of St Joseph were participating in the cross-congregational dialogue on the tenets of religious life facilitated by the establishment of the Canadian Religious Conference (CRC) in 1954. As Heidi MacDonald's chapter in this book details, the CRC gave Canadian men and women religious a unique forum for discussing critical ideas and concepts. In contrast to many other jurisdictions, including their American compatriots, the members of the CRC were not segregated by canonical status, sex, or language. The CRC represented both men and women religious, nuns and sisters, priests and brothers, diocesan and pontifical congregations, English and French. It established committees, sponsored research, launched journals, and commissioned a number of publications in which the Sisters of St Joseph participated and gave leadership.

Mother St Brigid Gillen, the superior general who received Bernadette Bouchard into the congregation and who oversaw her transformation into Sister Mary Alban, was an active participant in the CRC. In 1956, Mother St Brigid Gillen penned an essay for the CRC series on vows. Her essay, "Religious Poverty," detailed a changing understanding of what the vow of poverty meant in contemporary religious life. She began with a reflection on the responsibilities of a superior:

> A superior's first duty is one of Charity to her subjects, and she must never make things more difficult than need be for them. She has an obligation to cultivate a Christ-like manner, kind and gentle without failing to be firm, never sarcastic, never making a personal issue out of an unusual request … All superiors would do well to read the Holy Father's address to Superiors General at the close of the Congress at Rome in 1952 … [in which he states] "You must be motherly in your outward manner, in your speech and in your writings (as quoted 8–9)"… superiors … must be careful not to make the practice of poverty an excuse for any lack of justice and charity.[22]

Mother St Brigid's essay also documented the impact of the changing nature of women's work on community life, especially the impact of the increased qualifications for professional work, and the need for sisters to care for themselves. She wrote, "a regular vacation may seem a great departure from tradition ... but I think that most of us are convinced that it is one of these departures that our times demand, one thing in which tradition must be sacrificed" – a sacrifice, she concluded, that would result in "the strengthening of the Community Spirit."[23] Sister Mary Alban benefited from the implementation of these changes. She enjoyed time at the sisters' vacation home, Invermera, and had opportunities to pursue higher education and earn further professional qualifications.

Thus, even before Pope John XXIII announced Vatican II and summoned his bishops to meet in council, the Sisters of St Joseph of Toronto were making changes to their community practices. The postwar baby boom led the community to assess their resources and plan for the expansion of their secondary school system. Sister Mary Alban was soon swept into these changes. Under the vow of obedience, she left the path of her career in the hands of her superiors, and yet she was caught off guard in 1958 when the community informed her that it had other plans for her: "After some years of teaching small children – who both reveal God and expose us – I was to be surprised by being taken from the classroom and sent to study at the University of Toronto (St Michael's College) the so-called 'Honours Course' in English Language and Literature. The four-year course covered just about everything in English literature from Anglo-Saxon times to the present (1960s)."[24]

The community had decided that Sister Mary Alban was to qualify as a secondary school teacher. Although Catholic high schools in Ontario did not receive funding beyond Grade 10, they were inspected by the Ministry of Education in order to grant to their pupils an Ontario Secondary School Graduation Diploma. Sisters teaching core senior subjects were required to hold undergraduate degrees. Thus, many communities, including the Sisters of St Joseph of Toronto, sent sisters to university to engage in full-time study. From 1958 to 1962, Sister Mary Alban was a full-time student. She lived at St Joseph's College, the congregation's residential Catholic women's college, as she took classes with both lay students and other religious who were pursuing degrees at the University of Toronto. She began her studies as the Second Vatican Council was called and graduated in the midst of its deliberations. Just as her educational path had been shaped by the changes in religious life that predated the council, the implementation of the changes mandated by the Council Fathers shaped her subsequent career and led her to live her life on a much broader canvas than she would have ever imagined.

Speaking on the fiftieth anniversary of the opening session of the Second Vatican Council, Pope Benedict XVI succinctly explained its purpose: "There were no particular errors of the faith to correct and condemn, nor were there specific questions of doctrine and discipline to be clarified … [rather] the faith had to speak with a 'renewed' and more incisive voice, because the world was changing rapidly, but it had to maintain its perennial message intact, without giving way or compromising."[25]

Under the leadership of two popes, John XXIII and Paul VI, the council met in four sessions from 1962 to 1965 to undertake the task of renewing the Church for a changing world. The council issued four constitutions, three declarations, and nine decrees.[26] While all the documents issued by the council played a role in the renewal, the implementation of two documents in particular, *Perfectae Caritatis* and *Lumen Gentium*, had a profound impact on the understanding and practice of religious life, and radically reshaped it. Ironically, the majority of the documents' authors were male secular priests – that is, priests who were not themselves members of religious congregations and did not live under the canonical vows of poverty, chastity, and obedience. Even more ironic, the documents were written by men, and the women religious who would be the most dramatically influenced by them did not have a voice in their creation nor were they permitted to vote on their adoption. Vatican II was a Church event that was created by men and whose active participants were men, leaving the voices and participation of the 50 percent of the Roman Catholic Church who were women both unrepresented and silent. The ten women religious who attended the third and fourth sessions of the council in 1964 and 1965 did so as auditors – that is, they merely listened. They did not speak, nor could they vote.[27]

The decree that had the greatest impact on these silent women religious auditors as well as Sister Mary Alban and her congregation was *Perfectae Caritatis*, issued in October 1965. The purpose of religious life, it declared, was "to help the members follow Christ and be united to God through the profession of the evangelical counsels. It should be constantly kept in mind, therefore, that even the best adjustments made in accordance with the needs of our age will be ineffectual unless they are animated by a renewal of spirit. This must take precedence over even the active ministry."[28]

Thus, like all its sister and brother congregations worldwide, the Sisters of St Joseph of Toronto was mandated to engage in renewal

– even if it came at the cost of their active professional work in education, social service, and health care. *Perfectae Caritatis* directed religious communities to "return to the sources of all Christian life and to the original spirit of the institutes and their adaptation to the changed conditions of our time."[29] It further instructed that the religious habit should be modified into one that was "simple and modest, poor and at the same time becoming. In addition it must meet the requirements of health and be suited to the circumstances of time and place and to the needs of the ministry involved."[30] The document highlighted the need for the appropriate preparation of teaching sisters for their professional roles in society, directing that "their religious and apostolic formation, joined with instruction in arts and science directed toward obtaining appropriate degrees, must be continued as needs require in houses established for those purposes."[31] Implicit also in the decree's pages was a reconceptualization of the vow of obedience. Rather than decision-making by fiat from the superiors and general council, congregations were to collaboratively engage in discussions of their roots and their operations. They were directed to "adjust their rules and customs to fit the demands of the apostolate to which they are dedicated,"[32] and the voice and wishes of the individual community members were to be considered as actions were taken.

As if the calls to action in *Perfectae Caritatis* were not complicated enough, when *Lumen Gentium* appeared a short four weeks later, it presented a more fundamental challenge to the understanding of what many held to be the nature of religious life. The sixth chapter read, "From the point of view of the divine and hierarchical structure of the Church, the religious state of life is not an intermediate state between the clerical and lay states."[33] Religious were not a third state. They were members of the laity. While the document went on to explain that the Synod "encourages and praises the men and women, Brothers and Sisters, who in monasteries, or in schools and hospitals, or in the missions, adorn the Bride of Christ by their unswerving and humble faithfulness in their chosen consecration and render generous services of all kinds to mankind,"[34] it left religious congregations asking: what place did religious occupy within the structure of the Church? For, if they were in fact members of the laity, what was to be their purpose and role?

Beginning in May 1967, the Sisters of St Joseph of Toronto launched the "endeavours for renewal." A series of papers were commissioned, institutes were established, speakers were appointed, and commissions were set up within the community to explore all forms of congregational

Figure 3.2 Sister Mary Alban in Marshall McLuhan's class, 1962. From the scrapbook entitled "My Sacred History. Sister Mary Alban Bouchard," Mary Alban Bouchard, CSJ, Personal Collection, CSJT Archives.

life and ministries. These activities would culminate in the General Chapter of 1968: a congregational meeting that would respond to the directives of Vatican II and at which the future of the congregation was determined. The commissions focused on a number of topics: the apostolic works of the community, administration and governance, community life, education (which explored the elementary, secondary, and post-secondary sectors), spiritual life, and initial and ongoing formation. Each commission was chaired by a sister who had experience in that domain. While three to five other sisters were named to each commission to assist the chair in the research, writing, and recommendations, all members of the congregation had the opportunity to participate in the data-gathering sessions, expressing their thoughts in large and small group sessions on the directions the community should undertake.

Sister Mary Alban experienced the first stirrings of Vatican II as a student at the University of Toronto. Her studies at St Michael's College brought her into contact with leading Catholic intellectuals and broadened her studies in literature and philosophy. She described this time as formative in her intellectual maturity, declaring that "good literature, next to the Sacred Texts, is the greatest school of humanity and can only serve to expand us and prepare us to accept our place in the human family and live it out to its full and unique significance."[35] One of her teachers at St Michael's College was Marshall McLuhan, a convert to Catholicism who even today occupies a central place in the field of media studies.

She was a devotee of McLuhan and his work, but not an uncritical one. She embraced the opportunities to engage on an intellectual level with emerging technologies and their social implications. Yet as a teacher and a writer, she wondered about the place of her passion for literary expression in this new world of media. She expressed her frustration after one seminar by returning to her favoured means of expression: poetry. She ended her reflective verse, *On Being a Poet*, with the lines

I have no technique
That equals my vision.
I'd succeed
If I only could make an incision
And open my world.
But I reach the vanishing point
Before I can make an appearance.
My genius is out of joint
I fail by the flaws of coherence.
Please advise – in lieu of the symbolique
Shall I try to write?
Or should I reverse the decision
Scrap my insight
And purchase a new television?[36]

As a Sister of St Joseph, Sister Mary Alban participated in the commissions and discussions that led up to the General Chapter of 1968. With her honours degree in English in hand, she entered the expanding Catholic secondary school network and began a ten-year career as a secondary school teacher. She taught in the two flagship schools of the community: St Joseph's Morrow Park and St Joseph's College School. Since 1854, the Sisters of St Joseph had operated a boarding and day school in their motherhouse, which for almost a century was located in downtown Toronto. Under the leadership of Mother Maura McGuire, the motherhouse was relocated to the northern limits of the city of Toronto, and a new, purpose-built complex that also housed a day and boarding school, to be known as St Joseph Morrow Park, was constructed. A new day school, St Joseph's College School, was built near the grounds of the former motherhouse, which was sold to the Government of Ontario and razed.

While teaching high school English at Morrow Park, Sister Mary Alban was given a new writing assignment by her superior general

– to work on writing a reading series for pupils in the primary and junior divisions.

Sister Mary Alban had always been a prolific writer. She kept a journal. She contributed to professional periodicals for teachers, including *The Basilian Teacher*, a publication of the Congregation of St Basil – the male religious order that had established St Michael's College School for Boys and the University of St Michael's College in Toronto, as well as a number of other schools and colleges across Canada and in the United States. In an article entitled "Poetic Reflection," she explained her writing process (and notably described the poet as male): "The poet must carry it until he releases it in a materialized form. This is why I said above that I do not think that everyone could live with that condition. Yet, I must confess to a certain sloth and procrastination. I often carry the burden rather than undertake the labor of bringing forth my creation. Let no one think a poet is a dreamer who never works. Making poetry is slave labor. One is, if he is a true poet, chained to his burden. Yet, like the Creator and like woman, he loves the fruit of his labor."[37]

Writing was both a joy and, because it elicited in Sister Mary Alban feelings of guilt, a burden. For a religious whose life was engaged in the active apostolate, and in a community where service in education, social service, and health care defined the sisters – and in their pre-Vatican II lives defined the colours of their habit (white as the colour of the work habits for sisters in health care working in the wards, black as the colour of the formal habits for sisters in administration, education, and social service) – writing brought conflicting feelings. She explained that

> I have learned that this is a common suffering of writers. I was writing a good deal for professional journals and magazines. I was writing poetry as I had done since I was a child. It was always my practice also to keep a journal especially since the Superior General of my early days had called me into her office one day and told me I was to keep what I wrote and not throw it out. Now I was let loose in the field of children's literature and given a mandate to produce creative reading experiences for children. It was another of those wonderful surprises that Providence offers us to expand and free and enlarge our hearts. It gave me thinking time, imagining time. Writing came naturally to me and it stirred not only my imagination, that maker of images, but also my creative unconscious which is the well of the Spirit's dwelling. It required and indicated a life of reflection. Creative writing and poetry are

> not prayer but require perhaps a predisposition for contemplation because of the seeing that takes place. This task I was given was another cause for gratitude.[38]

Mother Maura McGuire, the superior general who assigned Sister Mary Alban to author school readers, encouraged a number of other sisters to develop their artistic talents, and to develop skills that would be considered outside those required in traditional institutional settings. For example, Mother Maura also encouraged Sister Dorothy Grills, a teacher and visual artist, to attend the Ontario College of Art to develop her skills as a painter. Considering the needs, interests, and abilities of the sister, not merely the needs of the congregation, was another feature of religious life in the post-Vatican II era.

Yet at the same time their religious life was being reshaped, so too was an institution in which many of the Sisters of St Joseph served: the school. Like many other pillars of society, education was affected by numerous seismic shifts during the 1960s – and perhaps nowhere more so than in the elementary sector. Research and findings in child development were reshaping approaches to literacy. To meet these changes, publishers launched new reading series and congregations of teaching sisters were logical partners to mine as a source of expertise. Richard Litch, the managing director of the Canadian elementary school textbook publisher Ginn and Company, wrote to Mother Maura McGuire to request her assistance in identifying a sister teacher to participate in the writing of "our new series of readers for separate schools." He explained that Ginn had enlisted the collaboration of many religious congregations, including the other congregation that operated academies and taught in the separate schools: The Institute of the Blessed Virgin Mary – more commonly known as the Loretto Sisters. Litch wrote that "The Lorettos have made a most outstanding contribution to the teaching of reading through Mother Clement … a Lady of Loretto … [who] has been released from her teaching duties to carry authorship." He noted that while other orders – notably, but not mentioned by name, the School Sisters of Notre Dame – had participated as writers, the Sisters of St Joseph had not. On the recommendation of John Bennett, the former inspector of separate schools in Toronto, Litch contacted Mother Maura to rectify this lacuna, adding, "it seems to us a great lack in our series of books not to have a teacher from St Joseph's Convent so far."[39]

Mother Maura was a highly skilled teacher and hospital administrator who had a knack for matching people and positions. Sister Mary Alban described how she was once again surprised to be plucked from her high school classroom and "'missioned,' by my [superior general], to write full time, i.e. with a publisher. It was significant for me because I am a writer but this has always entailed a kind of guilt, as if it is not an 'apostolic work' but time furtively stolen from it, as it were." The opportunity to engage in this type of "apostolic work" was actually a strategic move on the part of Mother Maura, and one very much in line with the order's intent to position itself as a leader in Catholic education.

Like Sister Mary Alban, the representatives of the publisher were surprised by this choice. They questioned her suitability on the grounds of practice and academic preparation. After an initial meeting with Sister Mary Alban, they detailed their concerns in a letter to Mother Maura:

> Sister [Mary Alban] explained that she had not participated actively in the primary school area for a matter of eight years. This caused us concern to the extent that we feel special provisions would have to be made for sister to reacquaint herself … [as] a great deal of ferment is currently taking place in primary reading not only in the more traditional text books but in new Canadian developed materials and also basic philosophy and approach … [Since the Institute for] Studies in Education is again offering a course in reading for advanced teachers … Sister could obtain considerable assistance from teachers presently teaching grade two … consideration might be given to the involvement of additional teachers on a part time basis.[40]

In her written response to the publishers, Mother Maura addressed these challenges, identifying Sister Mary Alban as a goal-oriented "idea woman," personally and professionally suited to the task:

> I realize your anxiety concerning Sister Mary Alban in regard to her experience in Grade 2 … we have in community a number of experienced teachers who have recently or are teaching Grade 2 but the choice of Sister Mary Alban was made because she is primarily an "idea woman" with a good literary background who is tireless in reaching an objective … we had thought of forming a committee of the teachers to work closely with Sister Mary Alban … Sister will be free in June to visit different classrooms and teachers and is already investigating ways and means. Sister Mary Alban will be free to take the course that you suggested.

Mother Maura concluded her letter by stating that while the community thought Sister Mary Alban was the right person for the task, she could in fact be replaced if there were further objections. She offered this suggestion: "If you feel when you next meet with Sister that another choice should be made, it will be quite agreeable to us."[41]

Not one to leave outcomes to chance, Mother Maura wrote to the inspector of schools who had initiated the contact between Ginn and her community, John Bennett, explaining her rationale for her selection of Sister Mary Alban. Writing a week after she corresponded with the publishers (and knowing that the publishers would be in touch with him), she used the same language to explain her decision to Inspector John Bennett: "While Sister is now a high school teacher she has taught in the lower grades. Sister has been chosen because we feel she has a fine background for this type of work and is an 'idea' woman. We shall appoint a Committee of experienced teachers to help her in the project."[42]

At the subsequent meetings with Ginn, Sister Mary Alban was assessed as a more than suitable candidate and thus she undertook a writing assignment that saw her contribute to textbooks, readers, and teaching manuals produced by Ginn and Company for over a decade. The contracts the community signed on her behalf indicate that between 1.5 and 2 percent of the total revenues from the sales of the series would come to the community. Writing under both her secular name, Bernadette Bouchard, and her name in religion, Sister Mary Alban, she was part of a team of authors who produced the Ginn Integrated Reading Program, the Light and Life Reading Series, and the Sharing Points in Language Arts collection. These books were used in public and separate schools from coast to coast. Perhaps the most iconic character appearing in any of the series was the beloved English sheepdog, Mr Mugs, who even today has a large following online.

Sister Mary Alban continued to write, to think, and to learn as she spent her days as a teacher of English in the single-sex boarding and day school, St Joseph Morrow Park. Even though the school was located on a spacious property some 25 kilometres from the core of the city of Toronto and served an all female student population mostly drawn from an advantaged population, it was not immune from the challenges of the 1960s. In her autobiography, Sister Mary Alban described how the larger societal changes and the changes in the Catholic Church impacted her teaching.

> We were living a time of social upheaval such as was exemplified in the drug cults that were entrapping our youth, our students. We experienced a new consciousness breaking upon us. As Catholic teachers, we turned to teaching about and trying to do justice as a basic demand of the gospel. We became involved in social concerns. This meant more extra-curricular activities, weekend student retreats out of the city, weekend live-in fasts of poverty awareness in solidarity with the hungry of the so called "Third World," summer excursions with students in service to Native reservations or remote mountain areas. We became pilgrims, stretching ourselves to the limit of endurance in the walkathons that raised money to share with the suffering.[43]

When she addressed the twenty-fifth anniversary reunion at St Joseph Morrow Park, she reflected on what her years teaching at the school had meant to her. She described how she attempted to actualize the congregation's vision for the education of girls and young women. The school took its motto from the Congregation of the Sisters of St Joseph of Toronto – "the love of Christ has gathered us together as one" – and its mission statement, even today, encapsulates that motto in the goals for its students:

> As a Catholic school
> We wish to continue the tradition
> Of a Christ-centered community
> Inspired by the Sisters of St Joseph
> Fostering in students academic excellence
> The desire for lifelong learning and personal growth
> While inspiring them to be respectful
> Just and socially responsible citizens of the world.[44]

Sister Mary Alban described the multi-segmented dreams that the sisters had for their pupils, each one framed by social justice initiatives and liberation theology. She urged them to become "REAL women … not the women in the ads: not the artificial women, the women who reveal that our society is dying of galloping consumption. Real women live in simplicity and with wisdom. Wisdom, you know, in the Scripture, the wisdom of God, is feminine and comes from the mouth of God. The real woman, and especially the real Christian woman, has the wisdom to know that our ego is not the centre of the universe: rather, there is a pearl of great price, a treasure buried within, worth selling everything to buy. The world needs such women today."[45]

She encouraged them to use their creativity – and to model their lives on those individuals the school held up to them: "We wanted you to be creative, to know your gifts and to use them for life. We knew you were all gifted – all. We held up before your eyes many models of persons who had lived their lives creatively,"[46] naming men and women, children and adults, Christians and non-Christians, lay and religious, citizens of the first and third world: "Mother Teresa, Gandhi, Martin Luther King, Anne Frank, Jean Vanier, Cardinal Léger, and especially Jesus ... God has shared God's own Spirit with each of you, that within you is a well and a fountain of living water. I say to you today, in the words of the Latin American theologian Gustavo Gutierrez, DRINK FROM YOUR OWN WELL [emphasis in original]. Let the wind blow through and the water flow."[47]

It is clear from these remarks that underpinning the overt and hidden curriculum she, as a teaching sister, delivered to the privileged young women in her classes was a social justice agenda, framed within a growing feminist consciousness, which grew from planned, practical activities, and from the motto of the congregation that also served as the motto for the school. Her career as a high school teacher sharpened her awareness of social inequities, leading her to request a transfer to the city core where she could engage more directly in social justice activities. She argued, "In the sixties, we strove to read the signs of the times. In the seventies, we began in earnest to read the signs on the interior road we were being called to travel."[48] And that road would take her, physically and practically, very far from both her privileged school and the security of living in a large community of sisters.

Influenced by her own readings and reflections, Sister Mary Alban found the atmosphere at the boarding and day school challenging. She was teaching a social justice agenda in her classroom, and outside school hours she worked with groups of male and female students in outreach activities: "Realizing that the environment in which I lived was a wealthy area of the city, that our students were drawn from there and from wealthy Latin American families who sent their daughters to our boarding school, and that the recently built and imposing 'mansion' that was our motherhouse was removed from the lives of the poor, I asked and was granted [permission] to move to the 'inner city.' I felt called more and more to go to the poor. I could hardly expect the poor to come to us in our suburban setting. I had to take the step to go where they were."[49] After close to a decade of teaching at Morrow Park, Sister Mary Alban moved to the congregation's downtown school, St Joseph's College School. Based there, she extended her social justice activities to include working with a diocesan priest, Father Tom McKillop. In 1966, McKillop had formed Youth Corps, an organization aimed at developing social justice leadership among Catholic teenagers and young adults. Sister Mary Alban worked on the weekend retreats, facilitated opportunities to work with disadvantaged populations, including the mentally challenged, and led student teams to visit and work in small and remote communities, including Indigenous communities in Ontario and in the interior of British Columbia.

Throughout her career as a teaching sister, Sister Mary Alban dealt with personal and professional challenges. She experienced the day-to-day challenges presented by teaching children and young women, and by living in the same shared space as her colleague sister-teachers. She had persistent physical ailments. Further, as did all women religious who persisted with their vocation throughout the turbulent 1960s and 1970s, she experienced profound sorrow as both men and women with whom she had entered religious life left. Yet, she persisted in her vocation and drew strength from finding God all around. She wrote,

> All things speak to us in a sacramental way of God's presence and action ... This is not pantheism for God is the creator, sustainer. And continuer of all is before all and above all and everything subsists in God ... It seems to me that, to brush such precious signs off as mere coincidences is to be blind, and worse, to deny God thanksgiving for such gracious actions toward us. Rather, it seems to me better that we become more and more sensitive to these small signs and find our awareness of and relationship to God enriched with tenderness, joy, gratitude and even strength and assurance.[50]

Through her study of world religions, she became more sensitive to the need for quiet time, for spiritual reflection and spiritual direction, and as she aged, she became more grateful for the time given over to spiritual retreats, such as the thirty-day Ignatian retreat, which she defined as a "tried and true method of spiritual challenge and growth."[51]

Sister Mary Alban's unstable health had always been one of her greatest challenges. She suffered from migraine headaches, caught pneumonia on an annual basis, and experienced a number of other physical ailments. In late 1973 and early 1974, she confided in her diary that she was "looking at the possibility of [her] own death."[52] In mid-January, she was diagnosed with an arterial blockage in her brain. She handled it with humour, writing "Nature is taking over – miraculously rerouting, redefining what it has to do ... I rest and smile because I am not going to die – yet."[53] She recovered and returned to teaching, but in the fall of 1974, her condition worsened again and she wrote in her diary, "I am terribly weak today, hardly able to walk ... I have to resign from my teaching position and enter hospital once more." She recorded the advice that her Youth Corps colleague Father Tom McKillop had given her: "Satan would have you abandon social justice and the efforts that have drained you ... take or live as much of that part of the Gospel that you are able."[54] She could not have realized at that time just how rapid and sustained would be her physical recovery, how quickly she would be launched onto an international stage, and how strongly, for the next almost forty years, her community would support her in a highly visible form of social justice activism – both in print and in person, at home and abroad.

As part of her recovery, she enrolled in the Divine Word International Centre for Religious Education in London, Ontario. Her studies furthered her theological education in liberation theology and introduced her to a network of individuals committed to peace and social justice. The Divine Word Centre was a product of Vatican II, the actualization of the vision of one of the Canadian bishops who played a significant role in both the deliberations of the council and the implementation of its initiatives: Gerald Emmett (later Cardinal) Carter. As an academic, a teacher, and a teacher educator, Carter was firmly committed to enhancing the quality of religious education provided within the Church. He structured instruction at the Divine Word Centre as graduate education and oversaw its successful affiliation with St Paul University in Ottawa, enabling graduates of the centre to receive a master's degree in religious education. The centre attracted scholars and students from across the world and established Canada's and Carter's reputation as leaders in religious education. For Sister Mary Alban, this was a transformative experience and she described it with the following metaphors that reflect her sensitivity to the environment: "I must add that many a time when I have found myself stalled or confined like a snake whose skin is too tight and has to be shed, or like the sprout of wheat just before it emerges above ground into the sunlight, or like the butterfly just before it breaks from the chrysalis; in other words, just at a growing point, I have noticed that I am presented with the chance to make good the moment."[55]

Her experience at the Divine Word Centre opened many paths. It brought her into new understandings of the theology of the Second Vatican Council; she was learning from scholars who were using techniques drawn from sociology and psychology to study religion and religious life; they would assist her in building new communities and networks with individuals who would guide her in an ongoing transformation from classroom teacher to activist. She lived in a residence with her fellow students, men and women drawn from many parts of the globe, and learned new meanings of community.

RELIGIOUS LIFE BEYOND VATICAN II: "WE ARE NOT LADIES IN WAITING. WE ARE WOMEN FOR PEACE."[56]

Sister Mary Alban left a classroom with four walls, but continued to teach through her words and her actions. On 10 August 1980, the Provincial Offences Court of the Judicial District of York issued a Probation Order for "Mary Alban" as a result of her conviction for an offence that occurred on 16 April 1980. The charge was that she "Fail[ed] to Leave Premises when required" and for that offence, she received a six-month suspended sentence, ordering her not to "commit the same offence or any related or similar offence ... [to] appear before the court as and when required ... [and to] notify the court of any change in his [*sic*] address."[57] What brought a woman religious, the author of a beloved primary reading series, and accomplished teacher of English to appear before the courts, to answer in the affirmative a charge of trespassing, and leave as a convicted criminal? In short, her formation as a peace activist.

Sister Mary Alban was born during the Depression, grew up under the shadow of the Second World War in the 1940s, became a teaching sister in the 1950s, and furthered her own religious and professional growth during the turbulent 1960s. In each of these decades, she was serving an apprenticeship that would lead her to a career as a peace activist. Her notes for the introduction to a manuscript on the United Nations contain the following reflections: "When I was very young a world war was being waged. And I was afraid. When it ended in 1945 in an atomic cloud of devastation, some people gathered in San Francisco and set up the United Nations organization. I thought: 'What a good idea! Now we will live in peace. Now there will be no more war in the world.'"[58]

She continued, describing how, on becoming a teaching sister, she "carried in [her] heart the burden of peace, the desire to educate for universal peace." The writings of Mahatma Gandhi on peace and non-violence led her to the conviction that "Gandhi had lived in a real and authentic way the moral teachings of Jesus Christ." While teaching at the motherhouse boarding school, St Joseph Morrow Park, she "inherited and fostered the United Nations Club" – which ultimately led her to work at the United Nations and to engage in peace activism and civil disobedience in both Canada and the United States.[59]

On 31 July 1976, Sister Mary Alban celebrated her Silver Jubilee – the twenty-fifth anniversary of her receiving the habit. Up to that time, she had had what one might describe as a conventional career as a teaching sister. As a novice, she attended normal school and began a career as an elementary teacher. Living under the pre-Vatican II norms of obedience, she had been posted to six elementary schools, spending terms of various lengths of time at each – from one month to four years. The leadership team of her congregation saw her strengths as a writer and a teacher, and invested in her further education. She was sent to study English and philosophy on a full-time basis, an action that spoke to the congregation's responsiveness to the needs of its growing involvement in the expanding secondary school sector. As a university student, she continued to publish in professional and congregational journals. Even as she taught English in secondary schools, she contributed to the Ginn reading series as well as writing other school texts. Her work at the private motherhouse school for privileged girls introduced her to the United Nations Clubs, and led her to diversify the curriculum she taught to include a strong emphasis on social justice.

A Jubilee Project, part of her Jubilee writings, is an apocryphal parable about a grapefruit tree:

> For my Jubilee year, I planted a grapefruit seed. I planted it three months ago in a little pot, which I labeled: "Mary Alban's grapefruit tree." I planted it and then began to hope. I don't know exactly why it became so important to me that it should grow. There's probably some Freudian explanation of misplaced motherhood. I watered it. I dug air holes in the soil. I put it in the sun and on dark days I put it under a lamp. I talked to it every day: "Grow, little tree." I told every one about it – every one who I thought would care. No doubt I was rather foolish about it. I watched and I waited. Most of all, I waited. It took so long but I never lost faith in the seed I had planted. At last a very tiny green stem appeared, so small that I was tempted to doubt it. But I waited. Then one day the tip of the stem seemed to be opening. I leaned over it and

> encouraged it. The next day it burgeoned into four tiny shiny leaves. I looked at it closely and I just couldn't resist saying: "You're beautiful!" And I told everyone: "It's growing! It's going to live and not die." The little tree is a parable of my life and I could wish that everyone might have touched the tree for a sign of the love and the care that has been spent by the One who watches over us.[60]

Just like the seed planted by Sister Mary Alban, the seed of social and environmental activism was casting out a network of roots and over the next twenty-five years would develop into something completely different. The changes brought about by Vatican II in the understanding of the vows, in congregational governance, and in the nature of religious life enabled Sister Mary Alban to enter a new phase of her life as a religious. In *Guidelines: The Special General Chapter 1968–9*, the Congregation of the Sisters of St Joseph highlighted the need to adapt its apostolic missions to the times. The *Guidelines* directed the sisters to acknowledge that

> The world of today calls for an adjustment of the Congregation to the changed conditions of the times ... Problems of poverty and social justice have always distressed religious women ... Some of our Sisters have felt drawn to missionary life ... to live among the poor in depressed areas ... to use their talents of mind in attacking the problems of poverty at the research or governmental level. The Congregation has accepted the principle therefore that Sisters may qualify for such positions as would allow them to share in the formulation of policy with regard to the poor and underprivileged both at home and abroad.[61]

After the health crisis that led Sister Mary Alban to resign from her work as a classroom teacher, she had been responding to the needs of the times by serving as a teacher beyond the walls of the classroom. She became actively involved with the original mandates of the Sisters of St Joseph of LePuy by working with the inmates at Warkworth Prison and in a storefront ministry to assist those living on the streets and in distress. She wrote that she had begun a new novitiate in active non-violence through her work in building support for the United Farm Workers' leafleting campaign. Her participation in that campaign brought her to an awareness of her passion for non-violence and disarmament.

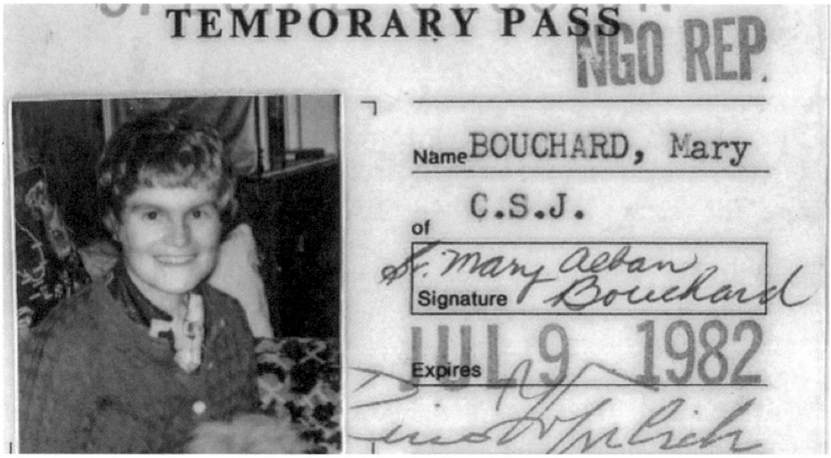

Figure 3.3 Mary Bouchard, United Nations temporary pass, 1982. From the scrapbook entitled "My Sacred History. Sister Mary Alban Bouchard," Mary Alban Bouchard, CSJ, Personal Collection, CSJT Archives.

Always a thinker – and in the words of Mother Maura, "an idea woman" – she began to act on her writings. Her work with youth and the marginalized brought her to view the intersectionality of peace activism and environmentalism. One of her first acts of overt peace activism occurred in October 1976, when she – with the support of her religious community – joined the thirty-day International Water Fast in front of the White House to protest the United States' growing involvement with nuclear arms. The following year, she journeyed from Toronto to Ottawa, completing a one-month walk for Peace and Life. She wrote an opinion piece, "Nuclear Suicide," in 1977, beginning with a quote from Sidney Lens, the author of *The Day before Doomsday*: "Either you will build a world in which war and exploitation become impossible or you will be the last generation." She ended by referencing the Old Testament: "What the peacemakers are asking on a very practical plain [*sic*], is what Yahweh asked in Deuteronomy 30:19: I CALL HEAVEN AND EARTH TO WITNESS THIS DAY THAT I HAVE SET BEFORE YOU LIFE AND DEATH, BLESSING AND CURSING: THEREFORE, CHOOSE LIFE THAT YOU AND YOUR DESCENDANTS MAY LIVE. [emphasis in original]."[62] She took this message on the real threat of nuclear suicide to all who would listen, speaking to service clubs, to student groups, to parish assemblies. The United Nations had always been a beacon of hope for her, and one that grew brighter through her involvement with the United Nations clubs as a secondary school teacher. In 1978, as an anti-nuclear activist, she attended the Special Session on Disarmament. Her experience there led her to request that her community leadership permit her to establish a new ministry: to serve as a non-governmental organization (NGO) representative to the United Nations.

She wrote a poem to commemorate her new mission:

AT THE UNITED NATIONS, NEW YORK 1979
It feels like a people's place
Of language and of face
Though there is rank and file
Man woman and child
Ambassadors and delegates
All the greats
Who here sit down
At tables found
No greater than you
Or I
Who try
To see
What we
Can make of this world
Our future or fate
There is nothing other to discuss
Or debate
Except this little earth
That has an expiry date.[63]

For the next ten years, with the exception of a sabbatical taken at the Poor Clares Monastery in Duncan, British Columbia, she attended sessions at the United Nations and co-founded and edited a monthly publication that was sent to religious congregations around the world. She staffed the prayer room and was "present." She produced documents for Global Education Associates, a New Jersey-based think tank founded in 1973 by Gerald and Patricia Mische as "a leading civil society organization working to educate for the emerging global context of human affairs."[64] She wrote extensively, publishing in a variety of venues including *Catholic New Times*, *Homiletic Services*, and the *Chelsea Journal*. She published three books through Novalis Press: *Peace Is Possible* (1985), *From Ashes to Light* (1987), and *Until the Son Is Risen* (1988). She took leadership roles in Pax Christi, an international organization for peace and social justice. While back in Toronto, she lived at her community's Matt Talbot House, a residence for recovering male alcoholics. She found that this experience resonated deeply within her: "In so many ways the struggles of the alcoholic men were so like my own – the repetitious pattern, the failures and successes, the discouragement and the revival."[65]

Even as she was entering her fourth decade in religious life, Sister Mary Alban found that she was being called to undertake another type of activity. She was no longer willing to be a commodity, in her words, "filling the need for a speaker for various groups and organizers of groups. (In our culture of consumerism, even spiritual and intellectual 'produce' becomes a commodity)."[66] She sought another type of mission, and through a pattern she had used before – prayer, retreat, and time to think – she found her answer. She explained: "In 1988, when I had been feeling for several months promptings to come to Haiti, promptings I could not dismiss, I felt the need of help to discern this movement in me. I chose to make the Canadian CSJ [Congregation of St Joseph] Federation retreat entitled: 'Growth in Discerning Love.' It was an important choice. The team whose members presented various topics were all our own sisters with training and experience to match the best of directors and they had their lived experience as Sisters of St Joseph to share as well."[67]

Thus, as a self-described reluctant missionary, she headed off to Haiti at age fifty-eight, and for the next twenty-four years engaged in a variety of social service and educational activities in Cap Haitien and Port au Prince. Haiti, the poorest country in the Western hemisphere, was in dire need of help – politically unstable, educationally deprived, and economically destitute. Many communities of religious, including the Sisters of St Joseph of Toronto, were supporting members of their communities to assist with social service initiatives, deliver health care, and provide educational support, especially by establishing literacy initiatives. Sister Mary Alban assisted with all three initiatives. She wrote sixteen booklets in Creole, a series entitled Lape Gaye (Sowing Peace), which served the dual purpose of enhancing literacy skills and encouraging the building of communities for peace. She continued to publish her writings and poetry, and in 1991 penned *Overcoming Loneliness Together: A Christian Approach* for Novalis Press. She assisted in the clinics operated by other religious communities. She built networks between and among people to encourage economic development. Collaborating with organizations and parishes in both Canada and the United States, Sister Mary Alban supported Haitian women in the creation of small businesses and encouraged the development of rental cooperatives. She worked with other religious congregations and participated in conferences to further her own intellectual growth. It was her attendance at one such conference that literally saved her life. On 12 January 2010, a magnitude 7 earthquake struck Haiti, flattening Sister Mary Alban's convent home. She was at a conference. She was evacuated to Canada on 23 January and returned to Haiti a few months later to assist in the rebuilding process. She would remain in Haiti, actively working in literacy programs, until her health failed her again. She was diagnosed with leukemia, returned to Toronto, and succumbed to the disease at the Sisters of St Joseph's new O'Connor Street motherhouse on 10 September 2013. She had time to reflect on her life, and to plan her funeral service – which, of course, featured her lifelong commitment to environmentalism and peace activism.

CONCLUSION

At the time of Sister Mary Alban's death, there were about 150 members of the Sisters of St Joseph of Toronto, less than a third of the number in 1965, the peak of membership. The congregation no longer administered a coast-to-coast network of schools, hospitals, and institutions of social service. It no longer recruited large classes – or bands – of postulants on an annual basis to replenish its numbers. Yet, as the 2015 Assembly of the Sisters of St Joseph in Canada proclaimed, "We are not finished yet … And neither is God."[68]

In designating 2015–16 as the Year of Consecrated Life, Pope Francis invited women and men religious to reflect on their purposes – both past and present: to review what they were called to do in the past, and to imagine their future. He issued this challenge to women religious:

> Recounting our history is essential for preserving our identity, for strengthening our unity as a family and our common sense of belonging. More than an exercise in archaeology or the cultivation of mere nostalgia, it calls for following in the footsteps of past generations in order to grasp the high ideals, and the vision and values which inspired them, beginning with the founders and foundresses and the first communities. In this way we come to see how the charism has been lived over the years, the creativity it has sparked, the difficulties it encountered and the concrete ways

> those difficulties were surmounted. We may also encounter cases of inconsistency, the result of human weakness and even at times a neglect of some essential aspects of the charism. Yet everything proves instructive and, taken as a whole, acts as a summons to conversion. To tell our story is to praise God and to thank him for all his gifts.[69]

Since the Second Vatican Council, many congregations have been actively analyzing their history and some have collaborated with secular scholars to do so. They have studied their charism and analyzed their governance structures in an attempt to learn from the past as they move to the future. In 2011, The *Constitutions* of the Sisters of St Joseph of Toronto were revised to reflect the ever-changing nature of religious life. The community defined its charism as "unifying love, as expressed by Father Medaille [the Jesuit priest who with six women founded the community], to bring about the total double union of ourselves and our neighbours with God, union of our neighbours among themselves and with us, but all in Jesus and in God."[70] Governance and decision-making is collegial, as is the assignment of tasks: "Each year the congregational leader missions each sister to a form of ministry through which it is possible for her to realize her part in the mission of the congregation and to use her gifts in the service *of the dear neighbor* [italics in original] … a ministry to which a sister is missioned by the congregational leader is a ministry of the congregation."[71] This transition from narrow, institutionally defined missions where sisters, under obedience, undertook without question the tasks assigned to them, to sisters who identified personal missions and sought congregational support for them can be seen in the career of Sister Mary Alban. While Vatican II led to radical changes in the operation, perception, and future of religious life, it is important to note that the changes it mandated were in fact accelerants to change that was already underway. Even before the Church Fathers gathered in council, the communities of religious themselves were exploring how their apostolates should intersect with the modern world.

The sisters who led the Sisters of St Joseph in the 1950s as superiors general were reading the signs of the times. In her essay on religious poverty, Mother St Brigid Gillen wrote of the need for superiors to exercise leadership as charity. She asked provocative questions about certain practices done in the name of poverty, suggesting that they may be mere annoyances that were undermining, rather than supporting, congregational community health. Mother Brigid saw the need to invest

Figure 3.4 Sister Mary Alban (1931–2013). From the scrapbook entitled "My Sacred History. Sister Mary Alban Bouchard," Mary Alban Bouchard, CSJ, Personal Collection, CSJT Archives.

in the education of teaching sisters in order to staff government-inspected high schools and sent young sisters, such as Sister Mary Alban, to acquire university degrees. Mother Maura McGuire saw talent in the young Sister Mary Alban and encouraged her to keep on writing. In spite of Sister Mary Alban's developing career as a secondary school teacher of English, Mother Maura identified her as a "woman of ideas" and put her forward to be a textbook writer for the Ginn publishing company.

Yet as social change occurred and as societal norms shifted, the Sisters of St Joseph supported their members as they moved in new directions.

As the study of theology opened to women, members of the Sisters of St Joseph, such as Sister Ellen Leonard, were among the first to obtain doctorates in that field and became leaders in new branches of study, such as the field of feminist theology. Even as their presence declined on university campuses – most notably the University of St Michael's College, as the Sisters of St Joseph closed their St Joseph's College Residence in 2007 – they established the Sisters of St Joseph's Chair in Systematic Theology at the Faculty of Theology. In the post-Vatican II period, as their numbers declined and the institutions they established and staffed came under lay control, the Sisters of St Joseph established partnerships with many Catholic, Christian, and secular organizations to carry out their charism of serving God through serving neighbour. Through sisters such as Sister Mary Alban, they became involved in international organizations, for example, the United Nations and Pax Christi. They partnered with activists such as Global Education Associates to advocate for peace. They became the public face and moral conscience of the nuclear disarmament movement by engaging in civil disobedience, for which they were brought before the courts. They educated the next generation of activists through their work in the school system, with social justice infusing the curriculum and opportunities for activism becoming features of extra- and co-curricular offerings. They participated in the leadership of Youth Corps. They engaged in adult faith education and faith development through their teaching and writings in the Catholic and secular presses. Internationally, involvement in the mission fields changed from congregationally based houses and institutions into collaboration with other religious communities and secular organizations. Through their financial support, their presence, and their advocacy, they exerted influence well beyond their numbers.

Sister Mary Alban was a complex woman. She was very human, finding both joy and pain, fulfillment and frustration, in living her life as a vowed religious. She loved her family – both those joined in blood and those joined by vows. She loved her God. She loved the earth and was fully committed to protecting it for the next generation. She chose as the central motif for her funeral mass one of her own compositions, "How Does the Earth,"[72] a call to environmental activism. Had she been alive on 24 May 2015, she would have rejoiced in the release of the encyclical letter *Laudato Si'*: On Care for Our Common Home. In it, Pope Francis takes the words of the canticle of St Francis to call for a dialogue to address "the urgent challenge to protect our common home … [and] to bring the whole human family together to seek a sustainable and integral development, for we know that things can change."[73] It captures in prose the same sentiments that she proclaimed in poetry and music.

The life and work of Sister Mary Alban illustrate the complexities and challenges that are created by the complex interactions of the reforms of Second Vatican Council and the social changes of the 1960s. The forces of feminism, social activism, and societal change cannot be separated from the changes in religious life. Sister Mary Alban lived in a community of women, and for a significant portion of her career taught girls and young women. Her actions and writings challenged both her sisters-in-community and her pupils. She challenged the graduates of Morrow Park to live as "REAL women … [with] the wisdom to know that our ego is not the centre of the universe."[74] She challenged the leadership of her community to support her in civil disobedience, social activism, and missions to which she felt personally called. Yet she undertook her activism as, and remained throughout her life, a member of both her faith community – patriarchal though it was – and her religious community, to which she looked for spiritual, financial, and emotional support.

Sister Mary Alban benefited from the wisdom of her predecessors – the leaders in the 1950s and 1960s who committed the community to the higher education of women. She benefited from the creation of cross-community initiatives such as the Canadian Religious Conference, which provided a safe forum for congregational leaders to share their concerns and formulate responses to challenges of the day. She also serves as an example of how individual and community activities are interwoven. She could not have lived the life she did without the support and resources provided by her religious community. Reciprocally, her religious community could not have responded to the needs of the times without the presence of a woman with such vitality and determination.

Conclusion

Rosa Bruno-Jofré, Heidi MacDonald, and Elizabeth M. Smyth

This book focuses on women congregations' encounter with modernity during the 1960s, 1970s, and 1980s. These three decades represent an era when social contentions revealed that paradigms no longer held and that new responses to both historical and emerging problems were required. The Western world was entering postmodernity, characterized by its fractured and liquid quality,[1] aptly characterized as an age of fracture, with the construct of woman being profoundly affected. A notion of identity common to all women was quickly problematized to a conception of womanhood that disaggregated along lines of race, gender, and sexuality. At the same time, the search for a personal and collective identity of religious communities was played out in a global and transnational arena; and in the background, the market ideology enjoyed unprecedented revival.

The book opens with the analysis of a collective enterprise, the Canadian Religious Conference (CRC), as a means to deal with the perfect storm of internal and external forces pressing on women's congregations. The CRC enabled women religious to reposition themselves as they rapidly declined in number from 66,000 to 44,127 between 1965 and 1975 due to the post-Vatican II tidal wave of dispensations from religious vows, as well as entrance rates falling far below rates of natural decrease. The threat of a parallel decline in influence was compounded by the withdrawal of women religious from hundreds of schools and hospitals, particularly in Quebec, where those institutions were targets of the Quiet Revolution. Their widespread resolution to forfeit their iconic habits in favour of secular dress, which made women religious indistinguishable from lay women, further contributed to the perception – and at least partial reality – that women religious had lost their pre-Vatican II authority.

Through the CRC, women religious joined their male counterparts to strengthen the influence of Canadian religious through consensus building and collective action. With an administrative staff of twenty-eight and an annual budget of $300,000 by 1976, the CRC built an effective organization with particularly strong research and communications departments. Without a doubt, they achieved their goal to be "the spokesman [*sic*] of religious life in Canada." Moreover, women religious were well served by their decision to be part of a national, mixed-gender organization – a decision that contrasted with American women religious who formed three separate women-only organizations. Their numerical domination of the CRC (75 percent of members were women religious) produced a feminist consciousness and feminist activism, demonstrated most notably in the CRC's submission to the Royal Commission on the Status of Women in 1967. This submission stressed the right of women to self-fulfillment regardless of their responsibilities to their husbands and children. The roughly equal number of female and male presidents of the CRC over several decades further suggests that women religious held a great deal of influence in the CRC, and the choice of the CRC not to take an anti-abortion stance suggests a level of progressivism that exceeded the official Church.

Following the CRC's example of repositioning through a collective organization, this book moves to the unique individual experiences of two women religious who were members of two distinct congregations, while focusing on the tensions emerging between efforts to build a community vision and personal experiences of faith. Our two protagonists, Sister Alice Trudeau, MO, and Sister Mary Alban Bouchard, CSJ, hovering over the tensions and searches inside the communities, read the positioning of the Church beyond its own set limitations and immersed themselves in the world to fully live the Gospel.

Sister Alice Trudeau is the focus of chapter 2. This chapter takes a *longue durée* approach to address the Oblate Missionary Sisters' complex process of resignification of vision and mission following Vatican II, in order to situate the prophetic feminist vision of Sister Alice Trudeau and its "failure" to be enacted in the congregation (she served as superior general from 1981 to 1989). Trudeau's personal journey and her spiritual testimonial work in Africa illustrate ways in which women and men religious encounter a plural world from a relativized position after Vatican II. It shows the embracing of a multidimensional sense of identity, malleability, and the construction of ways of living a liberating spirituality. This journey is examined using various conceptual tools. For example, Pierre Bourdieu's concept of field helps to explain the interactive forces and divisions in the community. Quentin Skinner's contextualist approach facilitates the understanding of the historical conditions feeding emerging intentionalities and of intentionalities themselves. A case in point is Trudeau's radical prophetic vision that went beyond the walls of the convent; she placed women's issues in relation to the clergy and the Church and envisioned a new way of dealing with power relations with the clergy. The notion of social imaginary from Charles Taylor becomes a heuristic tool to explore the barriers the congregation and Trudeau encountered in the process of redefining the community as a collective self. Not less important is the spiritual path followed by Trudeau: her pursuit of existential freedom and personal growth (Carl Rogers through André Rochais), Ignatian spirituality, and Christian meditation; and her powerful conviction of the relationship between social justice and faith.

From the example of Trudeau's failure to lead her congregation to accept her vision (and version) of Vatican II renewal, the book moves to an example in chapter 3 of a rank-and-file sister whose life in religion covered the second half of the twentieth century. Sister Mary Alban Bouchard spent her first twenty-five years in religious life as a teaching sister. Her congregation identified her intelligence and her innate talents as a writer. Initially, she was sent for further education to meet congregational needs. As the fields of study open to women religious broadened, Sister Mary Alban was able to study theology, thus gaining a network that furthered her deep commitment to peace activism and social justice. Sister Mary Alban's long life as a religious developed in three stages – teaching sister, social activist at home, and social activist abroad. At each stage, even as she engaged with broader communities beyond her convent walls, she viewed her community of religious sisters as her primary and fundamental pillar of support.

More than twenty years ago, Micheline Dumont published a significant study of Quebec women religious based on the question (and also her title), *Les Religieuses sont-elles féministes?*[2] In many ways, she was reconsidering Marta Danylewycz's argument in *Taking the Veil: An Alternative to Marriage, Motherhood, and Spinsterhood in Quebec, 1840–1920*, that many women religious in Quebec, especially those in leadership positions, were feminists, and in fact, the feminist and career opportunities provided by vowed life in Quebec had siphoned off so many potential leaders of a Québécois feminist movement that the movement was delayed in Quebec compared to other Canadian provinces. Dumont concludes that her question about whether women religious were feminists could be answered with either a yes or a no. Among the paradoxes of Quebec women religious, Dumont noted that although they had great influence in teaching a majority of Quebec schoolchildren, by monopolizing the teaching profession, they prevented many young lay women from having teaching careers, and through their mostly unremunerated work encouraged low wages for all working women in Quebec, an obviously "non-feminist" consequence. Dumont reflects that women religious have become increasingly feminist since the 1960s.[3] This is, in some ways, where our book begins. Very importantly, however, we explore the complexity beyond *whether* women religious were (or are) feminists.

The explosion of feminist analysis since Danylewycz's groundbreaking *Taking the Veil* was published almost three decades ago has led to new understandings of feminism in line with a range of beliefs related to gender equity and influenced by intersectionality. Such analysis is apt for studying women religious whose various perspectives, including their ethnicities, individual and congregational class backgrounds, levels of education, congregational charisms, and particular experiences in their work and spirituality (including, for example, degree of identification with liberation theology, feminist theology, or eco-spirituality) – not to mention their relationship with the larger Church – influence their beliefs and actions. While we avoided naming particular strains of feminism in the three main chapters of this book, we have illuminated varied examples of women religious' feminist *strategies* among our subjects. These women, members of communities of women, struggled with their identities in a patriarchal organization in a variety of ways and with different and fluctuating levels of feminist consciousness and *realpolitik*. In a way, the chapters speak to multiple feminisms in the same way we talk of multiple modernities.[4] In each chapter, it is clear that the reception and adaptation of concepts and issues from the feminist movement and feminist epistemologies were mediated by the transitional conditions of the congregations in the process of change. Despite the tide of hope among women religious that Vatican II would facilitate a broadening of their scope in the institutional church, Vatican II documents were ultimately silent on gender issues.

Our chapters illustrate how in spite of institutional constraints, women religious enacted agency, arising from a renewed reading of the Gospel, a commitment to social justice, and an awakening of their sense of personhood and search to reconstruct their communal and personal identity. Chapter 1 on the CRC demonstrates a remarkable commitment to gender solidarity; with such diversity in the almost two hundred women's congregations belonging to the CRC, the united voice was achieved only because so many women religious agreed to overlook their personal idiosyncrasies for the greater good of seeking women's improved status in the Church. The solidarity allowed the building of the Canadian Religious Conference as a medium for women religious to legitimize their voices in search for change and a new reading of the world. As the chapters on Alice Trudeau and Mary Alban Bouchard illustrate, education in liberation theology and engagement with social justice agendas brought both individual sisters and their congregations to question their identity as women within the Church. Chapter 2 documents that Alice Trudeau understood the workings of power, albeit intuitively, while Lea Boutin, also a superior general, wrote critically about patriarchy a few years after Trudeau's leadership. Chapter 3 illustrates how Sister Mary Alban displayed agency as a committed individual with support from the congregation, while Trudeau tried to move her congregation to embrace a new vision of the apostolate as women of faith committed to social justice and equality. These feminist biographies are key to understanding the complexity of feminism among women religious. As historical sociologists Glen Elder and Lisa Pellerin argue, "History makes its impress on a cohort one individual at a time. Without an understanding of the process by which that impress is made and a direct effort to model process, studies may result in only tables of inexplicable correlations."[5]

To date, few biographies exist of Vatican II-era women religious, but Geraldine Anthony, SCH, published a notable one in 1997 on Sister Irene Farmer. In 1962, Farmer became the congregational leader of the Sisters of Charity, Halifax, the largest English-speaking congregation of women religious in Canada, guiding the congregation through its most tumultuous period, and also serving as vice-president of the Women's Division of the CRC from 1969 to 1971.[6] In the same way feminist analysis has advanced since the publishing of Danylewycz's and Dumont's important books, so too has feminist biography evolved in the last twenty years. Anthony stresses that Farmer's determination to lead her congregation through a particularly progressive renewal process, despite the emotional trauma of being blamed for the congregation's financial demise and falling membership, was sustained by Farmer's almost hagiographic faith and vocation. Interestingly, Anthony relates Farmer's actions throughout her life to first and second wave women's rights advocacy but is never conclusive about Farmer's own "brand" of feminism. Today, twenty years after Anthony's biography was published, we aim for a more multidimensional approach toward Sister Alice Trudeau and Sister Mary Alban, but we continue to avoid categories of feminism.

We would argue that while the actions of the individual women religious and their communities may not be identified by a particular form of feminism, their actions can be seen as demonstrative of a particular reception of central feminist tenets. The tenets reached the congregations through the reading of feminist thinkers, writers, and theologians, with their distinctive methodological tools nourished by a different set of questions, a new positioning as women of faith, and a new epistemology involving new ways of knowing and new knowledge. Feminist theologians – both secular and women religious – went beyond the questions of women's exclusion from ordination, an issue not resolved yet. In the end, we conclude, based on the research conducted and reported here, that the epistemic break was not translated into dramatic changes in the status of women religious within the Church beyond modernizing governance, habits, and ways of being religious. The Vatican exercises ultimate power over congregations of women religious – and, as the Apostolic Visitation of Institutes of Women Religious in the United States of America, which issued its Final Report on 16 December 2014, illustrates, even fifty years after the end of Vatican II, questions of feminism and gendered identity are still very topical.

This book makes manifest the great opening that Vatican II meant in the life of the Church and, in this case, in religious congregations. The creation of the CRC shows that women and men religious acknowledged the inevitability of change and desired to deal with it head-on. The book also shows the role of institutional boundaries – residual elements from the past and from the gendered and hierarchical qualities of the Church as institution – evident in chapter 2. Chapters 2 and 3 offer detailed examples of the reception of Vatican II in two congregations and the corresponding effect that could have on individual sisters' lives, that is, the lived experience of Vatican II. The case of the Oblate Sisters and Sister

Alice Trudeau in chapter 2 shows that there could be great differences in the openness to, interpretation of, and response to Vatican II within congregations. While Trudeau herself was strongly in favour of profound transformations, many members of her congregation simply were not. In contrast, chapter 3's case study of Sister Mary Alban demonstrates the vastly changed opportunities for an individual sister whose congregation supported *Perfectae Caritatis's* call to return to the original mandate of the community and was able to successfully confront the challenges that both the individual and the collective would experience in responding to the needs of changing times.

The contrast in chapters 2 and 3 – between two sisters whose lives were affected so differently by their congregations' response to Vatican II renewal – shows the role of institutional boundaries that came from residual elements of the past (evident in chapter 2) and from the gendered and hierarchical qualities of the Church as institution in the renewal process. The book illustrates in vivid ways, and without neglecting feelings and desires, the paths individual sisters chose in their interactions with overlapping societal and ideological contexts.

The conceptual framework of the book provides the reader with an understanding of the collective – the CRC that became for female congregations a powerful voice for proposing changes – and with historical insights into the personal struggles and lived experiences of women religious belonging to two different congregations. These religious assumed roles beyond the regular spaces of action of their communities, enjoying the liberating effects of "living the radicality of the Gospel." And yet, as chapters 2 and 3 demonstrate, not all religious communities were elastic enough to support individual ministries, and not all religious spurred on by a highly personalized response to the radicality of the Gospel were able to successfully broker a working relationship within the communities that initially both shaped that drive and formed the response to it.

This book deals with tensions between the building of a collective congregational identity and the individual as salient individual religious without repressing differences. Religious identity as gender identity is compounded and differentiated by different ways of living spirituality and reading the world. Full participation in collective organizations comprising both men and women religious, and the pursuit of women's issues within them, adds another layer to the complexity involved in the interaction between institutional Catholicism and feminist causes.

Notes

INTRODUCTION

1 Marwick, *The Sixties: Cultural Revolution in Britain, France, Italy and the United States, c. 1958–1974*. As the title indicates, the long 1960s extends from 1958 to 1974.
2 The phrase "age of fracture" is taken from Daniel T. Rodgers, *The Age of Fracture*.
3 See McLeod, *The Religious Crisis of the 1960s*.
4 Rodgers, *Age of Fracture*, 39.
5 Bruno-Jofré, "Our Lady of the Missions (RNDM) in Canada, the Long 1960s, and Vatican II."
6 Lessard and Montminy, *The Census of Religious Sisters in Canada*, 274. Canadian Religious Conference, "CRC Statistics: 1975 Compared to 2004," http://www.crc-canada.org/sites/default/files/files/Stats%202011-2012.pdf.
7 See figure 1.3, this volume.
8 Canadian Religious Conference, "Statistics of the Religious Congregations of Canada," 2002, 28, A7, Canadian Religious Conference Archives (CRCA), Montreal.
9 Routhier, "The Second Vatican Council."
10 Hewitt, "Feminist Frequencies: Regenerating the Wave Metaphor."
11 Cooper, "The Convent: An Option for Québécoises, 1930–1950."
12 Danylewycz, *Taking the Veil*, 133.
13 Ebaugh, *Women in the Vanishing Cloister*, 133.
14 Rodgers, *Age of Fracture*, 39.
15 Quoted in Ebaugh, *Women in the Vanishing Cloister*, 133.
16 Smyth, "Professionalization among the Professed"; Smyth, "Sister Colleges: Women Religious and the Professoriate"; Fitzgerald and Smyth, eds, *Leading Women*; Smyth, "Gender, Religion and Higher Education."

17 See, for example, Bruno-Jofré, "The Missionary Oblate Sisters of the Sacred Heart and Mary Immaculate (MO) and the Sisters of Our Lady of the Missions (RNDM)."
18 Bruno-Jofré, "The Spiritual Journey of Alice Trudeau, MO."
19 Mangion, *Contested Identities*; Wittberg, "Called to Service."
20 Leonard, "The Process of Transformation"; Ruether, "The Emergence of Christian Feminist Theology"; Ruether, *Women-Church*.
21 Bruno-Jofré, "The Spiritual Journey of Alice Trudeau."
22 Pope Leo XIII, *Rerum Novarum*; Shannon, "*Rerum Novarum*."
23 Pope Pius XI, *Quadragesimo Anno*; Hinze, "*Quadragesimo Anno*."
24 Bruno-Jofré and Zaldívar, "The Center for Intercultural Formation."
25 Pope John XXIII, *Mater et Magistra*; Pope Paul VI, *Gaudium et Spes*.
26 Hollenbach, "Commentary on *Gaudium et Spes*."
27 Bruno-Jofré and Zaldívar, "The Center for Intercultural Formation."
28 "Oeuvre des religieuses dans l'ouest," *Chroniques des Missionnaries Oblates* 2, nos 1 and 2 (September–December 1914), reproduced from R.P. Lewis, OMI, *Les Cloches de Saint-Boniface* 8, no. 22 (15 November 1909), quoted in Bruno-Jofré, *The Missionary Oblate Sisters*, 137.
29 See Moyn and Sartori, "Approaches to Global Intellectual History"; Bruno-Jofré, *The Religieuses de Notre Dame des Missions*.
30 Bruno-Jofré develops this theme in her current research on Our Lady of the Missions and on the Sisters of the Infant Jesus (Spanish province).
31 Eustace et al., "American Historical Review Conversation."
32 For example, the Religieuses de Notre Dame des Missions. See "RNDM Earth Community: We Are One. We Are Love," 26th RNDM Congregational Chapter (Pattaya, Thailand, 18 January–15 February 2008), http://www.rndm.org/spirituality.aspx?sez=3&sotSez=6#115.
33 Bruno-Jofré addresses this issue in *The Religieuses de Notre Dame des Missions*, in progress.

CHAPTER ONE

1 See, for example, Ebaugh, *Women in the Vanishing Cloister*, chapter 6.
2 Lessard and Montminy, *The Census of Religious Sisters in Canada*, 274.
3 Ebaugh, *Women in the Vanishing Cloister*, 46–7.
4 The primary research for this chapter was drawn from the Canadian Religious Conference Archives, which comprises dozens of metres of archival material that were housed at Jean-Léon Allie Library and Archives of St Paul University in Ottawa when I used them but were

moved to CRC offices in Montreal in 2016. After receiving permission from the CRC, I visited the archives on three occasions between 2012 and 2015, focusing on (a) published material, such as the quarterly *CRC Bulletin* and numerous reports, (b) national and regional assembly materials, including committee and department reports, minutes, and summaries of keynote addresses, presentations, and workshops, and (c) press releases to the Catholic and secular presses in French and English Canada. The volume and quality of material allowed me to assess the role of the CRC and its evolution over six decades. Many thanks to Francine Cabana who coordinated my permissions with the CRC, and to Daniel Hurtubise, St Paul University Archivist, who provided crucial guidance in understanding the organization of the collection.

5 Philippe Sylvain, "Ignace Bourget," *Dictionary of Canadian Biography* (Online), http://www.biographi.ca/en/bio/bourget_ignace_11E.html.

6 "CRC Statistics – As of January 1st, 2004," CRC press release 15 February 2010, http://www.crc-canada.org/wp-content/uploads/2017/02/Stats-2011-2012.pdf

7 See page 163, endnote 26, this volume.

8 Paul VI, Decree on the Adaptation and Renewal of Religious Life (*Perfectae Caritatis*), 28 October 1965.

9 Paul VI, *Perfectae Caritatis*, # 4.

10 "and that all members be consulted in the preparation of the chapters of renewal." See Paul VI, *Ecclesiae Sanctae II*, 6 August 1966, #1– 3.

11 Chittister, *The Fire in These Ashes*, 171.

12 McKenna, *Charity Alive*, 194.

13 The number of Sisters of Charity, Halifax, fell from approximately 1,700 sisters in 1965, to 1,332 in 1975, to 413 today. See McKenna, *Charity Alive*, 101; Canadian Religious Conference, *Statistics of the Institutes of Consecrated Life and the Societies of Apostolic Life of Canada*, *1975 and* 2002, 31–2, 25–8; Sisters of Charity, Halifax, "Congregational Membership Lists," 1975–2011, Sisters of Charity, Halifax Archives.

14 Lessard and Montminy, *Census of Religious Sisters*, tables V and VI. The number of teachers was calculated by adding the 30,855 sisters Lessard and Montminy identified with 2/3 of the number they identified in the combined educators and Hospitaliers category (2/3 of 22,301).

15 Cellard and Pelletier, *Faithful to a Mission*, 170, 199.

16 Vayda and Deber, "The Canadian Health-Care System: A Developmental Overview," 131.

17 "First Order of Sisters in Canada" (1985), 4, non-accessioned box, Canadian Religious Conference Archives (CRCA), St Paul University, Ottawa.

18 Manzer, *Public Schools and Political Ideas*, 78.
19 Ibid., 166.
20 Ibid.
21 Before Vatican II, sisters rarely had any input into their work assignments. In interviews, sisters have often told me they did not like the work they were assigned to, and/or felt unqualified to do it.
22 Perhaps even more than the instability caused by changing goals and congregational identities was the "disappearance" of women religious on a weekly basis as women religious of various ages decided to return to secular life in a process where they were not allowed to say good bye to any other sisters or even disclose to them their thoughts of leaving. Anecdotal evidence of sisters waiting to see who *would not* show up at breakfast shows the high level of anxiety in the convent during the post-Vatican II years. Congregational leaders' decision to forbid any discussion of leaving with one's peers created a deep and unhealed wound within many women religious I interviewed.
23 For example, until 1984 Catholic schools in Ontario were only funded until grade 11, so women religious often subsidized the higher grades.
24 Before the introduction of the act, five provinces began to subsidize costs through universal insurance. See Vayda and Deber, "The Canadian Health-Care System," 127–8.
25 In Nova Scotia, for example, this was part of the argument the Sisters of Charity and the Sisters of St Martha used when they sold their hospitals to the province. They explained their long-term subsidization of building costs, in particular. See McKenna, *Charity Alive*, 287; and Cameron, *And Martha Served*, 297.
26 "Editorial," *Guardian* (Charlottetown, PEI), 21 December 1975.
27 Dickinson and Young, *A Short History of Quebec*, 307.
28 See Gidney and Millar, *How Schools Worked*, 4; Manzer, *Public Schools and Political Ideas*, 167–8.
29 Canadian Religious Conference, "Report of CRC to Holy See," *11th Annual Assembly*, 1965, 1, A–7, CRCA.
30 McKenna, *Charity Alive*, 69.
31 Ibid., 242.
32 Martin, "From Object of Poverty to National Treasure," 45–61. CEGEP is an acronym for Collège d'enseignement général et professionnel.
33 Wittberg, *From Piety to Professionalism and Back*, 69.
34 Ibid., 102.
35 Ibid., 184.

36 For criticism of the secularization thesis, see Smith, ed., *The Secular Revolution*, 14–17; as referred to in Wittberg, *From Piety to Professionalism*, 16n93; as well as Garnet et al., *Redefining Christian Britain*.
37 Brown, "Gender, Christianity, and the Rise of No Religion," 42.
38 Garnett et al., *Redefining Christian Britain*, 6.
39 Ibid., 12.
40 Taylor, *A Secular Age*, 489.
41 Abrams, "Mothers and Daughters," 62.
42 Ibid., 80.
43 Routhier, "The Second Vatican Council: A New Pentecost for the Church," 2; Lessard and Montminy, *Census of Religious Sisters*, Appendix; CRC, Women's Division, "Brief to the Royal Commission on the Status of Women presented by the Women's Section of the Canadian Religious Conference," 1968, B6, Box 2, CRCA.
44 Ebaugh, *Women in the Vanishing Cloister*, 82.
45 Wittberg, *From Piety to Professionalism*, 183.
46 Gläsel, "The Influence of Vatican II on Female Religious Orders."
47 Lévesque, "Deviant Anonymous."
48 Titley, "Recruitment to Catholic Religious Sisterhoods in the U.S., 1945–1965."
49 This was especially the case in interviews with the Presentation Sisters in Newfoundland in June 2013.
50 Starting in the 1950s, some congregations formed federations between larger groups with a common founder, such as the Sisters of Charity. Professional associations of teachers and specialized hospital professions also brought together sisters from different congregations.
51 "Health of a Sister," 14–17, CRC National Assembly, 1957, 14, C1, CRCA.
52 Ibid.
53 Owram, *Born at the Right Time*, 111–53.
54 CRC National Assembly, 1957, 18, CI, CRCA.
55 "Short History: [Canadian Religious Conference, 25 Years to 1979]," CRCA.
56 CRC National Assemblies, 1968–73, A4, Box 4–5, CRCA.
57 "Long Term Objectives," CRC National Assembly, 1968, iii, A4, Box 4, CRCA.
58 National Assembly, 1966, 3, A4, Box 4, CRCA.
59 "Short History," CRCA.
60 Of the staff, two were religious seconded from their congregations to work at the CRC and a third was an administrative support secular person.

61 CRC National Assemblies, 1969–76, Box 4–7, CRCA.

62 "Short History," CRCA. The founding of the CRC could be considered part of the renewal that is more associated with Vatican II. In 1962, for example, the women's side of the CRC discussed religious chastity, including whether "wrong ideas" about religious chastity were responsible for a variety of failures in religious life. A workshop in 1964 addressed "The Alienation of Property Belonging to Religious Communities," and focused significantly on hospitals. See CRC Assembly, 1962, "First Series of Questions for First Meeting in Committees," A4, Box 1, CRCA; and CRC, "Workshop: The Alienation of Property," August 1964.

63 Parsons, *Fifty Years of the Canadian Religious Conference*, 20.

64 Some belonged to American groups such as the Leadership Conference of Women Religious (LCWR) if any of their members served in the United States.

65 Male religious would have had better connections with episcopal authority than women religious could have, with the exception of those mother superiors who had male relatives in the episcopacy.

66 Parsons, *Fifty Years of the Canadian Religious Conference*, 21.

67 CRC National Assembly, 1972, "English Minutes," 6, A4, Box 5, CRCA.

68 CRC National Assembly, 1965, 4, A4, Box 3, CRCA.

69 CRC, "Census Returns of Sisters, Preliminary Report," 1965, Foreword, C1, Box 5, CRCA.

70 CRC, "Census Return of Sisters, Supplement to the Preliminary Report," 1965, Foreword, C1 Box 5, CRCA.

71 CRC, "Supplement to the Preliminary Report," 7–9.

72 The preliminary and supplementary reports were expanded again and published by the CRC as *The Census of Religious Sisters in Canada* in 1965. I am unclear on how broad distribution was at the time.

73 "A Brief Report of the Assessment Committee, CRC National Assembly," 1972, 45, CRCA.

74 "Statistics of the Religious Congregations of Canada," 1972, 53, CRCA.

75 Ibid., 53–5. They nevertheless "presupposed" that the number of new entrants would be 5 per 400 professed members and that there would be 20 percent attrition among new entrants. In fact, it was much worse.

76 "Statistics of the Religious Congregations of Canada," 1975, 2, CRCA.

77 "Statistics of the Religious Congregations of Canada," 1977, Introduction, CRCA.

78 Current and former women religious have repeatedly told me that the most educated left in larger numbers because they had more career and economic opportunities, and therefore easier transitions in returning to secular life.

79 "Long Term Objectives," iii, CRCA.

80 At the time, most congregations in Canada had papal status, which, in effect, allowed them self-government, because the Vatican was too busy to supervise them. Dozens of congregations in Canada were founded as diocesan congregations by local bishops, and these bishops held higher authority than the congregation's own mother superior. Experience with meddlesome local bishops led most of these congregations to seek papal status, which was preferred overall, but left no formal structure between the congregation and the local bishop. Diocesan congregations, of which there were relatively few in the post-Vatican II era, were significantly under the control of their diocesan bishop because their mission was to serve the diocese.

81 CRC General Assembly, 1964, 10, A4, Box 3, CRCA.

82 CRC General Assembly, 1968, 32–3, A4, Box 4, CRCA.

83 "A Brief Report of the Assessment Committee, CRC National Assembly," 1972, 11. This became article 2.1 in CRC Statutes.

84 "CCC– CRC Joint Reply to SCRIS on Relations between Bishops and Religious," *CRC Bulletin* 15, no. 5 (August–September, 1975): 6, A4, Box 5, CRCA.

85 Ibid., 6

86 Ibid., 7.

87 Ibid.

88 CRC General Assembly, 1984, 29, A4, Box 5, CRCA.

89 "Prospective: The CRC and Religious Life in Canada," CRC General Assembly, 1968, 31, A4, Box 3, CRCA; CRC, "Short History."

90 CRC National Assembly, 1972, 4, A4, Box 5, CRCA.

91 "The Prophetic Role of Religious Life," *CRC Bulletin* 16, no. 1 e 1, A4, Box 5, CRCA.

92 "Questionnaire accompanying Sister Ella M. Zink's comments to Sisters concerning the Brief to be submitted to the Royal Commission on the Status of Women," 29 November 1967, B6, Box 2, CRCA.

93 Sister Ella M. Zink, "Comments to Sisters concerning the Brief to be submitted to the Royal Commission on the Status of Women," 29 November 1967, B6, Box 2, CRCA.

94 Ibid.
95 "Brief to the Royal Commission," 12–15.
96 Bégin, "The Royal Commission on the Status of Women in Canada," 35.
97 "Brief to the Royal Commission," 16–18.
98 Evans, "The Women's Movement in the United States in the 1960s," 66.
99 "Brief to the Royal Commission," 17.
100 Berthelet, "Thinking Things Out," CRC *Bulletin* 24, no. 1 (January–March 1984): 6, A4, Box 5, CRCA.
101 CRC General Assembly, 1978, 21, 101, A4, Box 5, CRCA.
102 CRC General Assembly, 1980, 15, A4, Box 5, CRCA.
103 "CRC–Atlantic Regional Assembly," June 1988, 2, A6, Box 1, folder 1, CRCA.
104 Archbishop James Hayes, "Women as a Gift," CRC *Bulletin* 23, no. 3 (1983): 4, A4, Box 5, CRCA.
105 Kenneth Briggs, "Vatican Threat on Abortion Ad Went to Signers," *New York Times*, 19 December 1984.
106 See Conférence religieuse canadienne/Canadian Religious Conference, at http://www.crc-canada.org/en/about-crc/who-we-are.

CHAPTER TWO

1 Bruno-Jofré, *Missionary Oblate Sisters*. The school crisis between 1890 and 1896, when provincial legislation abolished confessional state-supported schools following the Laurier-Greenway Compromise, is known as the Manitoba School Question. The crisis had national repercussions. The Manitoba School Question was a Catholic question but also a French one, since the new legislation moved the Franco-Manitoban minority to the margins of power by denying French-speaking Manitobans the constitutional rights and privileges they had enjoyed earlier as members of a founding nation. See Perin, *Rome in Canada*.
2 "Alice Trudeau was born in a small Manitoba town, Île-de-Chênes, the youngest of fifteen children, in a Franco-Manitoban rural Catholic community. Her mother died when she was nine and her father when she was eleven … She was uprooted, separated from her immediate family, and, in her words, she was a 'lost child' who left behind security, love, and warmth. After living with an uncle and aunt, she moved in with her sister, Thérèse, when she was fifteen to help her take care of nine orphan children and a chronically ill sister, Rolande. Alice Trudeau found refuge in God to deal with the death and pain around her, and with her own pain. At age seventeen, while involved as leader in the Catholic Action movement, she fell in love with the young male president, who

proposed to her. However, after a prolonged inner struggle, she decided to choose religious life instead and entered the Missionary Oblate Sisters in August 1953. She was eighteen … When she joined the sisters, she brought with her an awareness of injustice as a Franco-Manitoban Catholic and her experience as an active member of the Catholic Action." Bruno-Jofré, "The Spiritual Journey of Alice Trudeau," 506.

3 The concept of *longue durée* comes from Fernand Braudel. See Braudel, *On History*, 25–54.

4 This chapter is a continuation of extensive research on the Missionary Oblate Sisters published in various places. I consulted primary sources and located the pictures in the archives of the missionary Oblate Sisters, the last time in August 2014. Pictures of paintings were taken in 2014. Provincial Superior Cécile Fortier and Sister Dora Tétreault provided new primary sources and pictures related to Africa during the writing of this chapter in the fall of 2015 and the winter of 2016. The materials will be returned to Fortier and Tétreault. Superior General Fortier provided written authorization for the use of the paintings and materials.

5 Bourdieu, *Language and Symbolic Power*.

6 Skinner, "Meaning and Understanding in the History of Ideas"; Tully, "The Pen Is a Mighty Sword."

7 Term originally coined by J.L. Austin and cited by Skinner, "Meaning and Understanding."

8 Taylor, *A Secular Age*, 171–2.

9 See, among others, Scott, "Gender: A Useful Category of Historical Analysis"; Miller, "Gender and Patriarchy"; Sue Morgan, ed., *The Feminist History Reader*.

10 See Rosa Bruno-Jofré and Ana Jofré, "Reading the Lived Experience of Vatican II."

11 Martel, *French Canada: An Account of Its Creation and Break-up, 1850–1967*, 1–4.

12 Term coined by Marwick. See Marwick, *The Sixties*, 7.

13 Fahrni and Rutherdale, *Creating a Postwar Canada*, 3; Fourastié, *Les Trente Glorieuses ou la révolution invisible de 1946 à 1975*.

14 Stevenson, "Developing Public Education in Post-War Canada to 1960," 386.

15 Bruno-Jofré, *Missionary Oblate Sisters*, 161.

16 Report of the Outgoing Superior General, Sr M. Jean-de-la-Croix, MO, General Chapter of July 1963, Archive of the Missionary Oblates (AMO).

17 The Archbishop of Saint-Boniface, Maurice Baudoux, who later participated in the Second Vatican Council, founded the Major Seminary. Sr Dora Tétreault, MO, provided the information.

18 Description provided to Sr Dora Tétreault by Sr Ghislaine Boucher.
19 Sr Cécile Fortier, MO, interviewed by Rosa Bruno-Jofré, 20 June 2008.
20 Report of the Outgoing Superior General, Sr M. Jean-de-la-Croix, MO.
21 Fondation Personnalité et Relations Humaines, *André Rochais: Founder of PRH*.
22 Bruno-Jofré, "The Process of Renewal of the Missionary Oblate Sisters, 1963–1989"; Fondation Personnalité et Relations Humaines, *André Rochais: Founder of PRH*; Personnalité et relations Humaines-International, *La personne et sa croissance*.
23 Delanti, *Social Theory in a Changing World*, 2.
24 See page 50 this volume.
25 Friedan, *The Feminine Mystique*; Hogan, *From Women's Experience to Feminist Theology*, 28–31.
26 Sr Dora Tétreault, comments made on 22 September 2006, written and deposited in AMO.
27 Sr Dora Tétreault, comments made on 22 September 2006; Sr Jeanne Boucher and Sr Lea Boutin, interviewed by Rosa Bruno-Jofré and Dora Tétreault, 26 October 1994, AMO.
28 Mounier, *Be Not Afraid*, *Personalism*.
29 Sr Dora Tétreault, comments made on 22 September 2006.
30 Ibid.
31 Sr Jeanne Boucher resigned in 1973; there was a chapter and elections but no report. Superior Lea Boutin's 1977 Report goes back to 1969. There was no report in between.
32 Actes du Onzième Chapitre Général de la Congrégation des Missionnaires Oblates du Sacré-Cœur et de Marie-Immaculée tenu à la Maison-Chapelle, Saint-Boniface, Manitoba, 10–22 July 1977, II, AMO.
33 Ibid., I.
34 Paul VI, Apostolic Exhortation of His Holiness Paul VI: *Evangelica Testificatio*, On the Renewal of the Religious Life According to the Teaching of the Second Vatican Council, 29 June 1971, http://w2.vatican.va/content/paul-vi/en/apost_exhortations/documents/hf_p-vi_exh_19710629_evangelica-testificatio.html.
35 Report of the Outgoing Superior General, General Chapter of July 1977, The Missionary Oblate Sisters of the Sacred-Heart and of Mary-Immaculate, Saint Boniface, Manitoba, 1977.
36 The Chapter refers to eleven sisters – from a total of 247 sisters – with problems of alcoholism and drug dependency, situations that are treated as medical and requiring personal commitment and community

support. The Chapter mentions that 5 percent of women religious in Canada and the USA were victims of the condition (Report of the Outgoing Superior General, General Chapter of July 1977, 33).

37 Report of the Outgoing Superior General, General Chapter of July 1977.

38 Decree on the Adaptation and Renewal of Religious Life (*Perfectae Caritatis*), in Abbott, *The Documents of Vatican II*, 2b.

39 Carmen Mangion's notion of contested identities as both agents and subordinated, active agents while distrusters of the world, provided a useful background to the analysis. Mangion, *Contested Identities*. Also, Nickie Charles, "Feminist Practices."

40 Pastoral Constitution on the Church in the Modern World (*Gaudium et Spes*), in Abbott, *The Documents of Vatican II*.

41 The superior general, Lea Boutin, referred to the Canadian bishops' efforts to call attention to social justice issues in Canada and in the third world in her report of 1977 (Report of the Outgoing Superior General, General Chapter of July 1977, 18). A Social Justice Committee was formed at the motherhouse, pamphlets and magazines were made available, and animators of Development and Peace gave information. The history of the Canadian bishops' involvement in social issues in Canada and abroad is analyzed by Baltutis, "Experimenting Creatively with Being Church in the Modern World."

42 See note 1.

43 For example, Sr Dora Tétreault, MO, "Notre oblation et l'esprit de reparation," manuscript written and presented to the congregation in February 1977, revised and corrected in January 1978. Sr Dora Tétreault, "The Spirit of Oblation and Reparation of the Missionary Oblate Sisters," 1981, AMO.

44 Sr Jeanne Boucher and Sr Lea Boutin, interviewed by Rosa Bruno-Jofré and Sr Dora Tétreault, 26 October 1994, AMO.

45 Sr Jeanne Boucher and Sr Lea Boutin, interviewed by Rosa Bruno-Jofré and Sr Dora Tétreault, cited by Bruno-Jofré, "The Process of Renewal of the Missionary Oblate Sisters"; Tétreault, "Notre oblation"; Tétreault, "The Spirit of Oblation." See also Bruno-Jofré, *Missionary Oblate Sisters*, chapter 6.

46 Sr Jeanne Boucher and Sr Lea Boutin interviewed by Rosa Bruno-Jofré and Sr Dora Tétreault, cited by Bruno-Jofré, "The Process of Renewal of the Missionary Oblate Sisters."

47 "Premières Constitutions des Soeurs Missionnaires Oblates du Sacré-Coeur et de Marie Immaculée" (1906), copy of the manuscript, Saint-Boniface, Manitoba, 3 July 1968, chapter 1, D9, 8, AMO, 16.

48 Constitutions and Modalities of the Congregation of the Missionary Oblates of the Sacred Heart and of Mary Immaculate, Saint-Boniface, 1983, article 3, 1.
49 Constitutions and Modalities, 2.
50 Wittberg, *The Rise and Fall of Catholic Religious Orders*, 256.
51 Ibid., 256.
52 Ibid., 252.
53 Ibid. Even the Second Vatican Council rejected calls to consider psychoanalysis. Interestingly, the Bishop of Cuernavaca, Mexico, Méndez Arceo, and Gregorio Lemercier – at the time, the prior of the monastery Santa María de la Resurrección in Santa María de Ahuacatitlán – made a presentation at the Second Vatican Council during discussion of Schema 13 on the Church in the modern world, asking that psychoanalysis be considered as relevant as the work of Darwin or Galileo. The proposal was rejected. See Bruno-Jofré and Zaldívar, "The Radicalization of Monsignor Ivan Illich's Critique."
54 Sr Dora Tétreault, personal communication; Sr Jeanne Boucher and Sr Lea Boutin, interviewed by Rosa Bruno-Jofré and Sr Dora Tétreault, 26 October 1994.
55 Boutin, *Women in the Church*.
56 Written communication from Sr Dora Tétreault, 15 August 2009.
57 Sr Alice Trudeau, "Dynamic Memory," typed manuscript, AMO.
58 Sr Alice Trudeau, "Personal Reflections" (on her personal style of accompaniment), manuscript provided by Dora Tétreault, property of the congregation, AMO.
59 Sr Alice Trudeau, "Personal Reflections."
60 Report of the Outgoing Superior General, General Chapter of 1981, Saint-Boniface, Manitoba, 2, 3, AMO.
61 Sr Alice Trudeau, interviewed by Rosa Bruno-Jofré and Sr Dora Tétreault, 21 October 1994, AMO.
62 See Daly, *The Church as the Second Sex* and *Beyond God the Father*.
63 See Ruether, *New Woman, New Earth*, "Envisioning our Hopes," "Feminist Interpretation of the Bible," and *Religion and Sexism*.
64 See Schneider, *Women and the Word*.
65 See Schüssler Fiorenza, *In Memory of Her*.
66 See Fiand, *Living the Vision*.
67 Sr Rose Marie Viallet, MO, interviewed by Sr Dora Tétreault, 28 March 2008, AMO.
68 Ibid.

69 Sr Alice Trudeau, MO, "Une religieuse interpelle les Oblats," typed manuscript, 1983, AMO.
70 Ibid., 1.
71 Ibid.
72 Ibid., 2.
73 Ibid.
74 Ibid.
75 Congrès Communautaire MO held in St Boniface, 4–15 July 1983. Also in the Capitular documents of the 13th General Chapter of the Missionary Oblate Sisters of the Sacred Heart and of Mary Immaculate, held at the Motherhouse, St Boniface, Manitoba, 4–25 July 1985, 13.
76 Alice Trudeau, "Onward in Hope," in Capitular documents of the 13th General Chapter of the Missionary Oblate Sisters of the Sacred Heart and of Mary Immaculate, entitled *Together in Hope*, held at the Motherhouse, St Boniface, Manitoba, 4–25 July 1985, 1–4.
77 Ibid., 4.
78 Ibid., 5.
79 Sr Rose Marie Viallet, MO, interviewed by Sr Dora Tétreault, 28 March 2008, AMO.
80 Congrès Communautaire MO held in St Boniface, 4–15 July 1983, 9.
81 Ibid., 10–11.
82 The MO Sisters' Congress produced a document entitled "Spiritual Formation of Youth and Adults" in which there is a long quotation from the survey conducted by the Canadian Religious Conference among bishops and published in *Donum Dei* 28 (1983): 263; Congrès Communautaire MO, 47–51.
83 Sr Alice Trudeau, interviewed by Rosa Bruno-Jofré and Sr Dora Tétreault, 21 October 1994, AMO.
84 Several sisters attended national Aboriginal conferences over a few years, as well as the international conference of Kateri Tekakwitha in 1983 and in 1984.
85 "Pastoral Work with the Amerindians," Congrès Communautaire MO, 43–6.
86 Ibid., 44.
87 Ibid.
88 Ibid., 43.
89 Sr Bernadette Boulet, MO, interviewed by Sr Dora Tétreault, 22 February 2008.
90 Sr Marie Anne Fillion, MO, interviewed by Sr Dora Tétreault, 26 February 2008.

91 Sr Dora Tétreault, interviewed by Sr Rose Marie Viallet, MO, 28 March 2008, comment made by Tétreault.
92 Sr Alice Trudeau, "Prophetic Leadership," manuscript, October 1988, AMO, 1–2.
93 Brueggemann, *The Prophetic Imagination*.
94 Ibid., 8–9.
95 Ibid., 4; Bruno-Jofré, "The Spiritual Journey of Alice Trudeau," 510.
96 Ensemble dans la fidélité, Compte-Rendu de l'Administration Générale de la Congrégation des Missionnaires Oblates du SC et de MI, Soumis au 14e Chapitre général tenu à St-Boniface, 9–25 July 1989, 5.
97 Ibid., 9.
98 Ibid.
99 Berger, *The Many Altars of Modernity*, ix, x.
100 II Conferencia General del Episcopado Latinoamericano. Documentos Finales de Medellin. http://www.celam.org/doc_conferencias/Documento_Conclusivo_Medellin.pdf. Accessed 25 May 2016.
101 Sr Alice Trudeau, MO, "Sentiers nouveaux pour demain," 1993, manuscript provided by Sr Dora Tétreault.
102 Desmarais, MSS, "La Restauración de las Fuerzas Vitales Humanas en la Experiencia Traumática" ; Sr Alice Trudeau, MO, Human Growth Session workshop, "Enhancing the Quality of Your Leadership through the Actualization of Your Vital Human Strengths," 12–19, September 1993, Montreal.
103 Desmarais, "La Restauración de las Fuerzas Vitales Humanas." Later IFHIM opened a project known as Aide à la Reconstruction des Personnes/Aid to the Reconstruction of Persons (ARP) that was implemented first in Goma, Zaïre (now Democratic Republic of the Congo), after the genocide in Rwanda in 1994, and then in Burundi as well as in Haiti.
104 Sr Alice Trudeau, "Processus d'Actualisation des Forces Vitales Humaines: Immersion II and III – 1991–1992," presented to Jeannine Guindon, December 1992, 102–3.
105 Sr Alice Trudeau, "Pédagogie de croissance humaine et spirituelle: Deux approches complémentaires," Congrés de spiritualité Ignatienne, 30–31 October 1993, in binder entitled *All What Alice Did between August 1993 to August 1994*, in Winnipeg, after IFHIM training.
106 Interview with Hélène Kilimnik, 30 August 1993; *All What Alice Did*.
107 "Reconstruction of the Person," personal spiritual notes by Sr Alice Trudeau. Handwritten manuscript provided to the author by Sr Dora Tétreault, dated 1994.

108 On 6 April 1994, when the plane carrying the Hutu president of Rwanda, Juvenal Habyarimana, was shot down, 800,000 civilian Tutsis were killed in ten weeks, in a low-tech intentional genocide. In July 1994, the extremist Hutu government was overthrown by the Tutsi-led Rwanda Patriotic Front; in the days that followed, one million Hutu refugees fled Rwanda to Zaïre (now Democratic Republic of the Congo), and half a million to Tanzania. The UN High Commissioner for Refugees established camps in Zaïre. Adelman, "Chaos in the Camps," 89.
109 Sr Alice Trudeau, interviewed by Rosa Bruno-Jofré and Sr Dora Tétreault, 21 October 1994, AMO, 36.
110 "Alice," manuscript dated 13 December 1994.
111 Congregation of the Missionary Oblate Sisters of the Sacred Heart and of Mary Immaculate, *One Little Seed.*
112 Ibid., 50.
113 Alice Trudeau and Cécile Fortier, "ARP: Un Souffle de Force Vitales," typed manuscript for distribution provided by Sister Dora Tétreault; Alice Trudeau and Cécile Fortier, "Á nos parents, amis, amies bienfaiteurs et bienfaitrices," debriefing of the mission in Goma, Zaïre, Équipe Ressource MO Saint-Boniface, Manitoba, 26 March 1997.
114 Trudeau and Fortier, "Á nos parents," 2.
115 Ibid.
116 Sr Marie-Marcelle Desmarais, cited in ibid., 2.
117 Trudeau and Fortier, "ARP: Un souffle."
118 Cécile Fortier and Alice Trudeau, "Projet d'aide à la reconstruction des personnes II, Masisi. Goma (République démocratique du Congo) du 1er mai au 26 octobre 1996," July 1997, IFHIM, 3.
119 Adelman, "Chaos in the Camps"; Thomas Olesen, "Global Injustice Memories"; Dallaire, "Looking at Darfur, Seeing Rwanda"; Lesnes, "Rwandan Killers and Refugees."
120 Adelman, "Chaos in the Camps," 90.
121 Ibid.
122 Binder containing faxes collected by Sr Cécile Fortier.
123 Binder containing faxes collected by Sr Cécile Fortier, 1.
124 Binder containing faxes collected by Sr Cécile Fortier, 4.
125 Trudeau and Fortier, "Á nos parents. The situation in the camps was dangerous."
126 For example, Sr Alice Trudeau to Sr Marie-Marcelle Desmarais, through Terre Sans Frontières, fax dated 16 October 1996. Binder containing faxes collected by Sr Cécile Fortier.
127 Adelman, "Chaos in the Camps," 89.

128 Ibid., 90.

129 Sr Marie-Marcelle Desmarais to Sr Alice Trudeau and Sr Cécile Fortier, through Terres Sans Frontières, fax dated 17 October 1996. Binder containing faxes collected by Sr Cécile Fortier.

130 Congregation of the Missionary Oblate Sisters of the Sacred Heart and of Mary Immaculate, *One Little Seed.*

131 Cécile Fortier and Alice Trudeau, "Projet de reliance-suivi auprès des multiplicateurs et multiplicatrices à la reconstruction des personnes. ARP III. Goma (République démocratique du Congo)," presented to Terre Sans Frontières and l'Institut de Formation Humaine Intégrale de Montréal, April 1998.

132 Trudeau and Fortier, "ARP: Un soufflé."

133 Ibid.

134 Safari, "Church, State and the Rwandan Genocide."

135 Ibid., 874.

136 Sr Alice Trudeau, MO, interviewed by Rosa Bruno-Jofré and Sr Dora Tétreault.

137 See Piiparinen, "Rescuing Thousands, Abandoning a Million."

CHAPTER THREE

1 Pope Francis, Apostolic Letter of His Holiness Pope Francis to all Consecrated People on the Occasion of the Year of Consecrated Life, 21 November 2015.

2 Carey, *Sisters in Crisis: The Tragic Unraveling of Religious Life*, 1997. Carey's second edition of this book is *Sisters in Crisis Revisited: From Unraveling to Reform and Renewal*, 2013.

3 In this chapter, congregation, order, and community are used as synonymous even though they are canonically distinct.

4 Miller, "Biographical Method," 16.

5 Banner, "Biography as History"; Booth, *How to Make It as a Woman*; Miller, *Researching Life Stories and Family Histories*; Chamberlayne, Bornat, and Wengraf, eds, *The Turn to Biographical Methods in Social Science*; Roberts, *Biographical Research*; Plummer, *Documents of Life 2*; Wengraf, *Qualitative Research Interviewing*.

6 MacMillan, *History's People*, 88.

7 Ibid., 158.

8 See, for example, Joyce Marshall, ed., *Word from New France*. Marie de l'Incarnation is also one of the three subjects in N.Z. Davis, *Women on the Margins*. Patricia Simpson has written extensively on Marguerite

Bourgeoys, including *Marguerite Bourgeoys and Montreal, 1640–1665* and *Marguerite Bourgeoys and the Congregation de Notre Dame, 1665–1670*. See also Rita McGuire's biography of the Grey Nuns' founder: *Marguerite d'Youville: A Pioneer for Our Times*. For some representative scholars writing on women religious in English Canada, see the chapters in Elizabeth M. Smyth, ed., *Changing Habits*.

9 The historiography in French Canada is much richer. See, for example, Colleen Gray, *The Congregation de Notre Dame*; Jack L. Little, "Charities, Manufacturers and Taxes."

10 Sister Mary Alban Bouchard, *West of the Third Meridian: Autobiography to 1994*, 11, personal papers, Congregation of the Sisters of St Joseph of Toronto Archives (CSJT).

11 Sister Mary Alban Bouchard, *Pieces of My Life*, 13, personal papers, CSJTA.

12 Sister Mary Alban Bouchard, *West of the Third Meridian*, 14, CSJTA.

13 *Constitutions of the Sisters of St Joseph of* Toronto, 1935, 1–2, CSJTA.

14 Ibid., 2.

15 Ibid., 5.

16 Ibid., 8.

17 Ibid., 126–7.

18 Ibid., 126.

19 Ibid.

20 Pope Pius XII, *Sponsa Christi* (Bride of Christ), 21 November 1950.

21 Gerlier et al., *Return to the Fountainhead*.

22 Mother St Brigid Gillen, *Religious Poverty*, 15.

23 Ibid.

24 Sister Mary Alban Bouchard, *West of the Third Meridian*, 17–18, CSJTA.

25 "Pope at Audience Summarizes Essential Purpose of Vatican II," *Catholic World News*, 10 October 2012, https://www.catholicculture.org/news/headlines/index.cfm?storyid=15857.

26 The documents issued by the Second Vatican Council are listed in the bibliography. For additional information, see http://stjosef.at/council/.

27 The auditors were Sisters Costantina Baldinucci (Italy), Claudia Feddish (United States), Cristina Estrada (Spain), Marie Henriette Ghanem (Lebanon), Mary Luke Tobin (United States), Marie de la Croix Khouzam (Egypt), Sabine de Valon (France), Juliana Thomas (Germany), Suzanne Guillemin (France), and Jerome M. Chimy (Canada). For a fuller discussion, see Carmel McEnroy, *Guests in Their Own House*.

28 Pope Paul VI, Decree on the Adaptation and Renewal of Religious Life (*Perfectae Caritatis*), 28 October 1965.

29 Ibid., 2.

30 Ibid., 17.
31 Ibid.
32 Ibid., 8.
33 Pope Paul VI, Dogmatic Constitution on the Church (*Lumen Gentium*), 21 November 1965, 43.
34 Ibid., 46.
35 Sister Mary Alban Bouchard, *West of the Third Meridian*, 17–18, CSJTA.
36 When McLuhan died in 1980, she wrote two entries in her journal:

New Year's Eve, 1980

Marshal McLuhan is dead – it sounds like a mistake – a false alarm.
Marshal McLuhan, my teacher, my friend, whose children were my pupils.
Marshall McLuhan, can he really be gone? Or will his tall gaunt
figure, with the shoulders slightly raised, sometime still be seen
walking up the aisle at noonday worship? Will we, sometime when we
least expect, catch the laugh of his eyes or the witty turn of
a word? I looked at that broad forehead in repose as he lay in wake
and I felt awe at all it had contained.

January 3, 1981

The funeral. It was bitter cold.
What right had I to feel so bereaved? What right to weep so
many tears? I have a throbbing headache. Well, Marshall, I don't begrudge
it to you. In fact, I'm going to inscribe your name in my litany of
saints – north-northwest.

(Sister Mary Alban Bouchard, personal papers, CSJTA.)

37 Sister Mary Alban Bouchard, "Poetical Reflections," *Basilian Teacher* [n.d.], 292, personal papers, CSJTA.
38 Sister Mary Alban Bouchard, *West of the Third Meridian*, 35, CSJTA.
39 R. Litch to Mother Maura, 11 February 1966, Sister Mary Alban Bouchard, personal papers, CSJTA.
40 John Main to Mother Maura, 23 March 1966, Sister Mary Alban Bouchard, personal papers, CSJTA.
41 Mother Maura to John Main, 5 April 1966, Sister Mary Alban Bouchard, personal papers, CSJTA.
42 Mother Maura to Inspector John Bennett, 15 April 1966, Sister Mary Alban Bouchard, personal papers, CSJTA.
43 Sister Mary Alban Bouchard, *West of the Third Meridian*, 29, CSJTA.

44 St Joseph Morrow Park Catholic Secondary School, *Parent Handbook 2015–16*, ii, https://www.tcdsb.org/schools/stjosephmorrowpark/SJMP_Parent-Guardian_Handbook/Documents/Parent%20Handbook%202014_2015.pdf.

45 Sister Mary Alban Bouchard, 25th Anniversary of St Joseph's Morrow Park [1985], Sister Mary Alban Bouchard, personal papers, CSJTA.

46 Ibid.

47 Ibid.

48 Sister Mary Alban Bouchard, *West of the Third Meridian*, 43, CSJTA.

49 Ibid., 37.

50 Ibid., 58, 59, 60.

51 Ibid., 57.

52 Sister Mary Alban Bouchard, diary entry, 14 January 1974, personal papers, CSJTA.

53 Sister Mary Alban Bouchard, diary entry, 18 January 1974, personal papers, CSJTA.

54 Sister Mary Alban Bouchard, diary entry, 8 October 1974, personal papers, CSJTA.

55 Sister Mary Alban Bouchard, *West of the Third Meridian*, 45, CSJTA.

56 Mary Alban Bouchard, *Peace Is Possible*, 140.

57 Probation Order, 10 August 1981, 505–1–08, Sister Mary Alban Bouchard, personal papers, CSJTA.

58 Sister Mary Alban Bouchard, "Introduction for the book on the UN," [n.d.], personal papers, CSJTA.

59 Ibid.

60 Sister Mary Alban Bouchard, *West of the Third Meridian*, 31, CSJTA.

61 Sisters of St Joseph, "Guidelines: The Special General Chapter 1968–9," 54–5, CSJTA.

62 Sister Mary Alban Bouchard, "Nuclear Suicide," undated and unsourced opinion piece [1977], personal papers, CSJTA.

63 Sister Mary Alban Bouchard, "New York, 1979," personal papers, CSJTA.

64 C. Yomko, "Worshipping the Ground We Walk On."

65 Sister Mary Alban Bouchard, *West of the Third Meridian*, 160, CSJTA.

66 Ibid., 73.

67 Ibid., 179.

68 "We Are Not Finished Yet … And Neither Is God," summary of the 2015 Assembly of the Sisters of St Joseph in Canada.

69 Pope Francis, Year of Consecrated Life.

70 Sisters of St Joseph of Toronto, *Constitutions and Directory* (Toronto: Sisters of St Joseph of Toronto, 2011), 1, CSJTA.

71 Ibid., 17.

72 Sister Mary Alban Bouchard, "How Does the Earth?," words and music by Mary Alban Bouchard, CSJ, copyright held by Sisters of St Joseph of Toronto, 1991, personal papers, CSJTA.
73 Pope Francis, *Laudato Si'*.
74 Sister Mary Alban Bouchard, 25th Anniversary of St Joseph's Morrow Park (1985), personal papers, CSJTA.

CONCLUSION

1 Bauman, *Liquid Modernity*.
2 Dumont, *Les religieuses sont-elles féministes?*
3 Malouin, "Review of *Les religieuses sont-elles féministes?*" 266–7.
4 Rosa Bruno-Jofré is working with the concept of multiple feminisms in relation to contextual influence and system responses in processes of reception in her book on the Religieuses de Notre Dame des Missions, presently in process. For multiple modernities, see Eisenstadt, "Multiple Modernities in an Age of Globalization."
5 Elder and Pellerin, "Linking History and Human Lives," 294.
6 Anthony, *Rebel Reformer Religious Extraordinaire*, 166.

Bibliography

ARCHIVES

Archives of the Missionary Oblate Sisters of the Sacred Heart and Mary Immaculate, Mother House, St Boniface, Manitoba. The archives have been recently donated to Le Centre du Patrimoine, operated by the Societé historique de Saint-Boniface, Manitoba.

Canadian Religious Conference Archives, Jean-Léon Allie Library and Archives, St Paul University, Ottawa. In 2016, the archives were moved to the CRC offices in Montreal.

Congregation of the Sisters of St Joseph of Toronto Archives.

DOCUMENTS OF THE SECOND VATICAN COUNCIL

Constitution on Sacred Liturgy (*Sacrosanctum Concilium*), 4 December 1963, http://www.cin.org/v2litur.html.

Decree on the Means of Social Communication (*Inter Mirifica*), 4 December 1963, http://www.cin.org/v2commun.html.

Dogmatic Constitution on the Church (*Lumen Gentium*), 4 December 1963, http://www.cin.org/vwhurch.html.

Decree on the Catholic Churches of the Eastern Rite (*Orientalium Ecclesiarum*), 21 November 1964, http://www.cin.org/v2east.html.

Decree on Ecumenism (*Unitatis Redintegratio*), 21 November 1965, http://www.cin.org/v2ecum.html.

Decree on the Pastoral Office of Bishops (*Christus Dominus*), 28 October 1965, http://www.cin.org/v2bishop.html.

Decree on the Adaptation and Renewal of Religious Life (*Perfectae Caritatis*), 28 October 1965, http://www.cin.org/v2relig.html.

Decree on Priestly Training (*Optatum Totius*), 28 October 1965, http://www.cin.org/v2priest.html.

Declaration on Christian Education (*Gravissum Educationis*), 28 October 1965, http://www.cin.org/v2educ.html.
Declaration on the Relation of the Church to Non-Christian Religions (*Nostra Aetate*), 28 October 1965, http://www.cin.org/v2non.html.
Dogmatic Constitution on Divine Revelation (*Dei Verbum*), 18 November 1965, http://www.cin.org/v2revel.html.
Decree on the Apostolate of Laity (*Apostolicam Actuositatem*), 18 November 1965, http://www.cin.org/v2laity.html.
Declaration on Religious Freedom (*Dignitatis Humanae*), 7 December 1965, http://www.cin.org/v2relfre.html.
Decree on the Mission Activity of the Church (*Ad Gentes*), 7 December 1965, http://www.cin.org/v2miss.html.
Decree on the Ministry and Life of Priests (*Presbyterorum Ordinis*), 7 December 1965, http://www.cin.org/v2minis.html.
Pastoral Constitution on the Church in the Modern World (*Gaudium et Spes*), 7 December 1965, http://www.cin.org/v2modwor.html.

BOOKS AND ARTICLES

Abbott, Walter M., SJ, ed. *The Documents of Vatican II*. New York: The American Press, 1966.
Abrams, Lynn. "Mothers and Daughters: Negotiating the Discourse on the 'Good Woman' in 1950s and 1960s Britain." In *The Sixties and Beyond: Dechristianization in North America and Western Europe, 1945–2000*, edited by Nancy Christie and Michael Gauvreau, 60–83. Toronto: University of Toronto Press, 2013.
Adelman, Howard. "Chaos in the Camps." *Bulletin of the Atomic Scientists* 58, no. 6 (November/December 2002): 88–93.
Anthony, Geraldine. *Rebel Reformer Religious Extraordinaire: The Life of Sister Irene Farmer*. Calgary: Detselig Enterprises, 1997.
Baltutis, Peter E. "Experimenting Creatively with Being Church in the Modern World: The Social Affairs Commission of the Canadian Conference of Catholic Bishops 1965–1984." In *Vatican II: Expériences canadiennes/Canadian Experiences*, edited by Michael Attridge, Catherine E. Clifford, and Gilles Routhier, 253–75. Ottawa: University of Ottawa Press, 2011.
Banner, Lois W. "Biography as History." *American Historical Review* 114, no. 3 (2009): 579–86. doi:10.1086/ahr.114.3.579.
Bauman, Zygmunt. *Liquid Modernity*. Cambridge: Polity Press, 2012.

Bégin, Monique. "The Royal Commission on the Status of Women in Canada: Twenty Years Later." In *Challenging Times: The Women's Movement in Canada and the United States*, edited by Constance Backhouse and David H. Flaherty, 21–38. Montreal & Kingston: McGill-Queen's University Press, 1992.

Berger, Peter. *The Many Altars of Modernity: Toward a Paradigm for Religion in a Pluralist Age*. Berlin: De Gruyter, 2014.

Booth, Alison. *How to Make It as a Woman: Collective Biographical History from Victoria to the Present*. Chicago: University of Chicago Press, 2004.

Bouchard, Mary Alban. *Peace Is Possible*. Ottawa: Novalis, 1985.

Bourdieu, Pierre. *Language and Symbolic Power*. Edited by John Thompson and translated by Gino Raymond and Matthew Adamson. Cambridge: Harvard University Press, 1991.

Boutin, Lea, MO. *Women in the Church: The Pain, the Challenge, the Hope*. Aurora: Emmanuel Convalescent Foundation, 1991.

Braudel, Fernand. *On History*. Translated by Sarah Matthews. Chicago: University of Chicago Press, 1980.

Briggs, Kenneth. "Vatican Threat on Abortion Ad Went to Signers." *New York Times*, 19 December 1984. http://www.nytimes.com/1984/12/19/us/vatican-threat-on-abortion-ad-went-to-signers.html.

Brown, Callum G. "Gender, Christianity, and the Rise of No Religion: The Heritage of the Sixties in Britain." In *The Sixties and Beyond: Dechristianization in North America and Western Europe, 1945–2000*, edited by Nancy Christie and Michael Gauvreau, 39–59. Toronto: University of Toronto Press, 2013.

Brueggemann, Walter. *The Prophetic Imagination*. Minneapolis: Fortress Press, 2001.

Bruno-Jofré, Rosa. *Missionary Oblate Sisters: Vision and Mission*. Montreal & Kingston: McGill-Queen's University Press, 2005.

– "The Missionary Oblate Sisters of the Sacred Heart and Mary Immaculate (MO) and the Sisters of Our Lady of the Missions (RNDM): The Intersection of Education, Spirituality, the Politics of Life, Faith and Language in the Canadian Prairies, 1898–1930." *Paedagogica Historica* 49, no. 4 (August 2013): 454–70.

– "Our Lady of the Missions (RNDM) in Canada, the Long 1960s, and Vatican II: From Carving Spaces in the Educational State to Living the Radicality of the Gospel." In *Catholicism and Education: Fifty Years after Vatican II (1962–1965), A Transnational Interdisciplinary Encounter*, edited by Rosa Bruno Jofré and Jon Igelmo Zaldívar, chapter 9. Toronto: University of Toronto Press, under review.

– "The Process of Renewal of the Missionary Oblate Sisters, 1963–1989." In Smyth, *Changing Habits*, 247–73.

– *The Religieuses de Notre Dame des Missions/Our Lady of the Missions* (RNDM) *in Canada (1898–2008): Women Religious as Educators at the Intersection of Locality, Identity Issues, and Transnational Configurations*. Book proposal approved by McGill-Queen's University Press, in progress.

– "The Spiritual Journey of Alice Trudeau, MO, in the Post-Conciliar Context." In *Vatican II: Expériences Canadiennes–Canadian Experiences*, edited by Michael Attridge, Catherine E. Clifford, and Gilles Routhier, 495–514. Ottawa: University of Ottawa Press, 2011.

Bruno-Jofré, Rosa, and Ana Jofré. "Reading the Lived Experience of Vatican II: Threading Words and Images, Contrasting with the Past, and Grasping the Spirit of the Times: The Oblate Sisters and the Sisters of Our Lady of Missions in Canada." Paper presented at Lived History of Vatican II Conference, University of Notre Dame, Indiana, 24–26 April 2014.

Bruno-Jofré, Rosa, and Jon Igelmo Zaldívar. "The Center for Intercultural Formation, Cuernavaca, Mexico, Its Reports (1962–1967) and Ivan Illich's Critical Understanding of Mission in Latin America." *Hispania Sacra* 64, extra II (July–December 2014): 457–87.

– "The Radicalization of Monsignor Ivan Illich's Critique of the Institutionalized Church and the Formation of Missioners, 1960–1966." *Journal of Ecclesiastical History* (forthcoming).

Cameron, James. *And Martha Served: History of the Sisters of St Martha of Antigonish, Nova Scotia*. Halifax: Nimbus, 2000.

Canadian Religious Conference (CRC). *Statistics of the Institutes of Consecrated Life and the Societies of Apostolic Life of Canada, 1975 and 2002*. Ottawa: Canada Religious Conference, 1975, 2002.

– *Statistics of the Religious Congregations of Canada*. Ottawa: Canadian Religious Conference, 1972–2002.

– "We Are Not Finished Yet … And Neither Is God." Summary of the 2015 Assembly of the Sisters of St Joseph in Canada. Video. http://www.crc-canada.org/en/node/1889.

Carey, Ann. *Sisters in Crisis: The Tragic Unraveling of Religious Life*. Huntington: Our Sunday Visitor, 1997.

– *Sisters in Crisis Revisited: From Unraveling to Reform and Renewal*. San Francisco: Ignatius Press, 2013.

Catholic World News. "Pope at Audience Summarizes Essential Purpose of Vatican II." *Catholic World News*. 10 October 2012. https://www.catholicculture.org/news/headlines/ index.cfm?storyid=15857.

Cellard, André, and Gérald Pelletier. *Faithful to a Mission: Fifty Years of the Catholic Health Association of Canada 1939–1989*. Ottawa: Catholic Health Association of Canada, 1990.

Chamberlayne, Prue, Johanna Bornat, and Tom Wengraf, eds. *The Turn to Biographical Methods in Social Science: Comparative Issues and Examples*. London: Routledge, 2000.

Charles, Nickie. "Feminist Practices: Identity, Difference, Power." In *Practising Feminism: Identity, Difference and Power*, edited by Nickie Charles and Felicia Hughes-Freeland, 1–37. London: Routledge, 1996.

Chittister, Joan. *The Fire in These Ashes: A Spirituality of Contemporary Religious Life*. London: Sheed and Ward, 1995.

Congregation of the Missionary Oblate Sisters of the Sacred Heart and of Mary Immaculate. *One Little Seed: A Hundred Years of History, 1904–2004*. Saint-Boniface: Missionary Oblate Sisters, 2004.

Cooper, Barbara J. "The Convent: An Option for Québécoises, 1930–1950." *Canadian Woman Studies* 7, no. 4 (Winter 1986): 31–5.

Dallaire, Roméo. "Looking at Darfur, Seeing Rwanda." *New York Times*, 4 October 2004. http://www.nytimes.com/2004/10/04/opinion/04dallaire.html.

Daly, Mary. *Beyond God the Father: Toward a Philosophy of Women's Liberation*. Boston: Beacon Press, 1973.

– *The Church as the Second Sex*. New York: Harper and Row, 1968.

Danylewycz, Marta. *Taking the Veil: An Alternative to Marriage, Motherhood, and Spinsterhood in Quebec, 1840–1920*. Don Mills: Oxford University Press, 1987.

Davis, N.Z. *Women on the Margins: Three Seventeenth-Century Lives*. Cambridge: Harvard University Press, 1997.

Delanti, George. *Social Theory in a Changing World: Conceptions of Modernity*. Cambridge: Polity Press, 1999.

Desmarais, Marie-Marcelle, CND. "La Restauración de las Fuerzas Vitales Humanas en la Experiencia Traumática." In *Sin lugar para ser humano: Intervención psicológica en crisis humanitarias, 10 y 11 de Abril de 2000*, edited by José M. Fernández Martos and Fátima Miralles Sangro, 47–68. Madrid: Universidad Pontificia de Comillas, 2000.

Dickinson, John, and Brian Young. *A Short History of Quebec*. 3rd ed. Montreal & Kingston: McGill-Queen's University Press, 2003.

Dumont, Micheline. *Les religieuses sont-elles féministes?* Montréal: Bellarmin, 1995.

Ebaugh, Helen Rose Fuchs. *Women in the Vanishing Cloister: Organizational Decline in Catholic Religious Orders in the United States*. New Brunswick: Rutgers University Press, 1993.

Eisenstadt, S.N. "Multiple Modernities in an Age of Globalization." *The Canadian Journal of Sociology* 24, no. 2 (Spring 1999): 282–95.

Elder, Glen H., and Lisa A. Pellerin. "Linking History and Human Lives." In *Methods of Life Course Research: Qualitative and Quantitative Approaches*, edited by Glen H. Elder and Janet Z. Giele, 264–94. Thousand Oaks: Sage, 1998.

Eustace, Nicole, Eugenia Lean, Julie Livingston, Jan Plamper, William M. Reddy, and Barbara H. Rosenwein. "American Historical Review Conversation: The Historical Studies of Emotions." *American Historical Review* 117, no. 5 (December 2012): 1487–530.

Evans, Sara. "The Women's Movement in the United States in the 1960s." In *Challenging Times: The Women's Movement in Canada and the United States*, edited by Constance Backhouse and David H. Flaherty, 61–71. Montreal & Kingston: McGill-Queen's University Press, 1992.

Fahrni, Magda, and Robert Rutherdale. *Creating a Postwar Canada: Community, Diversity, and Dissent, 1945–75*. Vancouver: University of British Columbia Press, 2008.

Fiand, Barbara. *Living the Vision: Religious Vows in an Age of Change*. New York: Crossroad, 1992.

Fitzgerald, Tanya, and Elizabeth M. Smyth, eds. *Women Educators, Leaders and Activists: Educational Lives and International Networks, 1900–1960*. Basingstoke: Palgrave Macmillan, 2014.

Fondation Personnalité et Relations Humaines. *André Rochais: Founder of PRH* (special edition of PRH-France 1991 Newsletter). Winnipeg: D.W. Friesen, 1994.

Fourastié, Jean. *Les Trente Glorieuses ou la révolution invisible de 1946 à 1975*. Paris: Fayard, 1979.

Francis I (pope). Apostolic Letter of His Holiness Pope Francis to all Consecrated People on the Occasion of the Year of Consecrated Life. 21 November 2015. https://w2.vatican.va/content/francesco/en/apost_letters/documents/papa-francesco_ lettera-ap_20141121_lettera-consacrati.html.

– *Laudato Si'*: On Care of Our Common Home. 24 May 2015. http://w2.vatican.va/content/francesco/en/encyclicals/documents/papa-francesco_20150524_enciclica-laudato-si.html.

Friedan, Betty. *The Feminine Mystique*. Harmondsworth: Penguin, 1963.

Garnett, Jane, Matthew Grimley, Alana Harris, William Whyte, and Sarah Williams, eds. *Redefining Christian Britain: Post 1945 Perspectives*. London: SCM Press, 2012.

Gerlier, Cardinal Peter, et al. *Return to the Fountainhead: Addresses at the Tercentenary Celebration of the Sisters of St Joseph Le Puy France*. St Louis: Sisters of St Joseph of Carondelet, 1950.

Gidney, R.D., and W.P.J. Millar. *How Schools Worked: Public Education in English Canada, 1900–1940*. Montreal & Kingston: McGill-Queen's University Press, 2012.

Gillen, Mother St Brigid. *Religious Poverty*. Ottawa: Canadian Religious Conference, 1956.

Gläsel, Kirsten. "The Influence of Vatican II on Female Religious Orders – Particularly on the Good Shepherd Sisters in Europe Alma." Paper presented at the Male and Female Religious and Vatican II International Colloquium, Rome, Italy, 14 November 2014.

Gray, Colleen. *The Congregation de Notre Dame: Superiors and the Paradox of Power*. Montreal & Kingston: McGill-Queen's University Press, 2007.

Hewitt, Nancy A. "Feminist Frequencies: Regenerating the Wave Metaphor." *Feminist Studies* 38, no. 3 (Fall 2012): 658–80.

Himes, Kenneth R., OFM, ed. *Modern Catholic Social Teaching: Commentaries & Interpretations*. Washington: Georgetown University Press, 2005.

Hinze, Christine Firer. "Commentary on *Quadragesimo anno* (*After Forty Years*)." In Himes, *Modern Catholic Social Teaching*, 151–74.

Hogan, Linda. *From Women's Experience to Feminist Theology*. Sheffield: Sheffield Academic Press, 1995, reprinted 1997.

Hollenbach, David, SJ. "Commentary on *Gaudium et Spes* (Pastoral Constitution on the Church in the Modern World)." In Himes, *Modern Catholic Social Teaching*, 266–92.

II Cònferencia General del Episcopado Latinoamericano. Documentos Finales de Medellín. http://www.celam.org/doc_conferencias/Documento_ Conclusivo_Medellin.pdf.

John XXIII (pope). *Mater et Magistra*: Encyclical of Pope John XXIII on Christianity and Social Progress. 15 May 1961. http://w2.vatican.va/content/john-xxiii/en/encyclicals/ documents/hf_j-xxiii_enc_15051961_mater.html.

Leo XIII (pope). *Rerum Novarum*: Encyclical of Pope Leo XIII on Capital and Labor. 15 May 1891. http://w2.vatican.va/content/leo-xiii/en/encyclicals/documents/hf_l-xiii_enc_15051891_rerum-novarum.html.

Leonard, Ellen, CSJ. "The Process of Transformation: Women Religious and the Study of Theology, 1955–1980." In Smyth, *Changing Habits*, 230–46.

Lesnes, Corine. "Rwandan Killers and Refugees: Among the Hundreds of Thousands of Hutu Who Fled to Tanzania Are Those Who Murdered Tutsi." *Le Monde*, 11 June 1994, 14.

Lessard, Marc A., and Jean-Paul Montminy. *The Census of Religious Sisters in Canada*. Ottawa: Canadian Religious Conference, 1965.

Lévesque, Andrée. "Deviant Anonymous: Single Mothers at the Hôpital de la Miséricorde in Montreal, 1929–1939." *Canadian Historical Association, Historical Papers* (1984): 168–84.

Little, Jack L. "Charities, Manufacturers and Taxes: The Montreal Sister of Providence Spruce Gum Syrup Case, 1876–78." *Canadian Historical Review* 95, no. 1 (2014): 54–77. doi: 10.3138/chr.1862.

Löwy, Michael, and Claudia Pompan. "Marxism and Christianity in Latin America." *Latin American Perspectives* 20, no. 3 (2013): 28–42.

MacDonald, Heidi. "'Sisterhood is Powerful': Feminisms inside and outside Congregations of Women Religious in Atlantic Canada." Paper presented at the Lived History of Vatican II Conference, University of Notre Dame, Indiana, 24–26 April 2014.

MacDonald, Stella, Sr. "Editorial." *Guardian* (Charlottetown, PEI). 21 December 1975, 4.

MacMillan, Margaret. *History's People: Personalities and the Past*. Toronto: University of Toronto Press, 2015.

Malouin, Marie-Paule. "Review of *Les religieuses sont-elles féministes?*" *Revue d'histoire de L'amerique francaise* 20, no. 3 (1996): 266–7.

Mangion, Carmen. *Contested Identities: Catholic Religious Women in Nineteenth-Century England and Wales*. Manchester: Manchester University Press, 2014.

Manzer, Ronald. *Public Schools and Political Ideas: Canadian Educational Policy in Historical Perspective*. Toronto: University of Toronto Press, 1994.

Marshall, Joyce, ed. *Word from New France: The Selected Letters of Marie de l'Incarnation*. Toronto: Oxford University Press, 1967.

Martel, Marcel. *French Canada: An Account of Its Creation and Break-Up, 1850–1967*. Canada's Ethnic Group Series, booklet no. 24. Ottawa: The Canadian Historical Association, 1998.

Martin, Tania. "From Object of Poverty to National Treasure: The Ambiguous Place of Catholic Convents in Quebec and the Rhetoric of Heritage." *Material Culture Review* 59 (Spring 2004): 45–61.

Marwick, Arthur. *The Sixties: Cultural Revolution in Britain, France, Italy and the United States, c. 1958–1974*. Oxford: Oxford University Press, 1998.

McEnroy, Carmel. *Guests in Their Own House: The Women of Vatican II*. Spring Valley: Crossroad, 1996.

McGuire, Rita. *Marguerite d'Youville: A Pioneer for Our Times: A Biography Based on the Life and Times of Marguerite d'Youville, Foundress of the Sisters of Charity (Grey Nuns) of Montreal*. Ottawa: Novalis, 1982.

McKenna, Mary Olga. *Charity Alive: Sisters of Charity of Saint Vincent de Paul, Halifax, 1950–1980*. Washington: Catholic University of America, 1998.

McLeod, Hugh. *The Religious Crisis of the 1960s*. Oxford: Oxford University Press, 2007.

Miller, Pavla. "Gender and Patriarchy." In *Handbook of Historical Sociology*, edited by Gerard Delanty and Engin F. Isin, 337–48. London: Sage, 2003.

Miller, Robert L. "Biographical Method." In *The A–Z of Social Research: A Dictionary of Key Social Science Research Concepts*, edited by Robert Miller and John D. Brewer, 15–17. London: Sage, 2003. doi:http://dx.doi.org/10.4135/9780857020024.
– *Researching Life Stories and Family Histories*. London: Sage, 2000.
Morgan, Sue, ed. *The Feminist History Reader*. London: Routledge, 2006.
Mounier, Emmanuel. *Be Not Afraid: Studies in Personalist Sociology*. New York: Harper, 1954.
– *Personalism*. Notre Dame: University of Notre Dame Press, 1952.
Moyn, Samuel, and Andrew Sartori. "Approaches to Global Intellectual History." In *Global Intellectual History*, edited by Samuel Moyn and Andrew Sartori, 3–32. New York: Columbia University Press, 2013.
"Oeuvre des religieuses dans l'ouest." *Chroniques des Missionnaries Oblates* 2, nos 1 and 2 (September–December 1914): 5–11. (Reproduced from R.P. Lewis, OMI. *Les Cloches de Saint-Boniface* 8, no. 22 [15 November 1909]). In Bruno-Jofré, *The Missionary Oblate Sisters*, 137.
Olesen, Thomas. "Global Injustice Memories: The 1994 Rwanda Genocide." *International Political Sociology* 6, no. 4 (2012): 373–89.
Owram, Doug. *Born at the Right Time: A History of the Baby Boom Generation*. Toronto: University of Toronto Press, 1996.
Parsons, Christina. *Fifty Years of the Canadian Religious Conference: An Overview*. Ottawa: Canadian Religious Conference, 2004.
Pastoral Constitution on the Church in the Modern World (*Gaudium et Spes*). In *The Documents of Vatican II*, edited by Walter M. Abbott, SJ. New York: The American Press, 1966.
Paul VI (pope). Apostolic Exhortation of His Holiness Paul VI: *Evangelica Testificatio*, On the Renewal of the Religious Life according to the Teaching of the Second Vatican Council. 29 June 1971. http://w2.vatican.va/content/paul-vi/en/apost_exhortations/documents/ hf_p-vi_exh_19710629_evangelica-testificatio.html.
– Decree on the Adaptation and Renewal of Religious Life (*Perfectae Caritatis*). 28 October 1965.
– Dogmatic Constitution on the Church (*Lumen Gentium*). 21 November 1965.
– *Ecclesiae Sanctae II*, 6 August 1966, #1–3.
– Pastoral Constitution on the Church in the Modern World (*Gaudium et Spes*). 7 December 1965.
Perin, Robert. *Rome in Canada: The Vatican and Canadian Affairs in the Late Victorian Age*. Toronto: University of Toronto Press, 1990.
Personnalité et Relations Humaines-International. *La personne et sa croissance: Fondements anthropologiques et psychologiques de la formation PRH*. Poitiers, France: Personnalité et Relations Humaines-International, 1997.

Piiparinen, Touko. "Rescuing Thousands, Abandoning a Million: What Might an Emancipatory Intervention Have Looked Like in Rwanda?" *International Relations* 21, no. 1 (2002): 47–66.

Pius XI (pope). *Quadragesimo Anno*: Encyclical of Pope Pius XI on Reconstruction of the Social Order. 15 May 1931. http://w2.vatican.va/content/pius-xi/en/encyclicals/documents/hf_p-xi_enc_19310515_quadragesimo-anno.html.

Pius XII (pope). *Sponsa Christi* (Brides of Christ). 21 November 1950. http://w2.vatican.va/c ontent/pius-xii/fr/apost_constitutions/documents/hf_p-xii_apc_19501121_sponsa-christi.html.

Plummer, Ken. *Documents of Life 2: An Invitation to Critical Humanism*. London: Sage, 2001.

Roberts, Brian. *Biographical Research*. Buckingham: Open University Press, 2002.

Rodgers, Daniel T. *Age of Fracture*. Cambridge: Harvard University Press, 2011.

Routhier, Gilles. "The Second Vatican Council: A New Pentecost for the Church." Canadian Religious Conference, 25 May 2012. http://www.crc-canada.org/sites/default/ files/files/VATICAN%20II%20Routhier.pdf.

Ruether, Rosemary Radford. "The Emergence of Christian Feminist Theology." In *The Cambridge Companion to Feminist Theology*, edited by Susan Frank Parsons, 3–22. Cambridge: Cambridge University Press, 2002.

– "Envisioning Our Hopes: Some Models of the Future." In *Women's Spirit Bonding*, edited by Janet Kalven and Mary Buckley, 325–35. New York: Pilgrim Press, 1984.

– "Feminist Interpretation of the Bible: A Method of Correlation." In *Feminist Interpretation of the Bible*, edited by Letty Russell, 111–24. Oxford: Basil Blackwell, 1985.

– *New Woman, New Earth: Sexist Ideologies and Human Liberation*. New York: Seabury Press, 1975.

– *Religion and Sexism: Images of Women in Jewish and Christian Traditions*. New York: Simon and Schuster, 1974.

– *Women-Church: Theology and Practice of Feminist Liturgical Communities*. Eugene: Wipf and Stock Publishers, 1985.

Safari, Peter C. "Church, State and the Rwandan Genocide." *Political Theology* 11, no. 6 (2010): 873–93.

Schneider, Sandra. *Women and the Word*. New York: Paulist Press, 1986.

Schüssler Fiorenza, Elisabeth. *In Memory of Her: A Feminist Theological Reconstruction of Christian Origins*. New York: Crossroad, 1987.

Scott, Joan Wallach. "Gender: A Useful Category of Historical Analysis." In *Gender and the Politics of History*, 28–50. New York: Columbia University, 1989.

Shannon, Thomas A. "*Rerum Novarum*." In Himes, *Modern Catholic Social Teaching*, 127–50.

Simpson, Patricia. *Marguerite Bourgeoys and the Congregation de Notre Dame, 1665–1670*. Montreal & Kingston: McGill-Queen's University Press, 2007.

– *Marguerite Bourgeoys and Montreal, 1640–1665*. Montreal & Kingston: McGill-Queen's University Press, 1997.

Skinner, Quentin. "Meaning and Understanding in the History of Ideas." *History and Theory* 8, no. 1 (1969): 3–53.

Smith, Christian, ed. *The Secular Revolution: Power, Interests, and Conflicts in the Secularization of American Public Life*. Berkeley: University of California Press, 2003.

Smyth, Elizabeth M. *Changing Habits: Women's Religious Orders in Canada*. Ottawa: Novalis, 2007.

– "Gender, Religion and Higher Education: A Century of Catholic Women at the University of St Michael's College." *Pedagogica Historica* 49, no. 4 (2013): 547–61.

– "Professionalization among the Professed." In *Challenging Professions: Historical and Contemporary Perspectives on Women's Professional Work*, edited by Elizabeth M. Smyth, Alison Prentice, Sandra Acker, and Paula Bourne, 234–54. Toronto: University of Toronto Press, 1999.

– "Sister Colleges: Women Religious and the Professoriate." In *Historical Identities: The Professoriate in Canada*, edited by Paul Stortz and E. Lisa Panayotidis, 207–24. Toronto: University of Toronto Press, 2006.

St Joseph Morrow Park Catholic Secondary School. *Parent Handbook 2015–16*. https://www.tcdsb.org/schools/stjosephmorrowpark/SJMP_Parent-Guardian_ Handbook/Documents/Parent%20Handbook%202014_2015.pdf.

Stevenson, Hugh. "Developing Public Education in Post-War Canada to 1960." In *Canadian Education: A History*, edited by J. Donald Wilson, Robert M. Stamp, and Louis P. Audet, 386–415. Scarborough: Prentice-Hall, 1970.

Taylor, Charles. *A Secular Age*. Cambridge and London: Belknap Press of Harvard University Press, 2007.

Titley, Brian. "Recruitment to Catholic Religious Sisterhoods in the U.S., 1945–1965." Paper delivered at the Canadian Historical Association Annual Meetings, Victoria, BC, 5 June 2013.

Tully, James. "The Pen Is a Mighty Sword: Quentin Skinner's Analysis of Politics." In *Meaning and Context: Quentin Skinner and His Critics*, edited by James Tully, 7–28. Cambridge: Polity Press, 1988.

Vayda, Eugene, and Raisa Deber. "The Canadian Health-Care System: A Developmental Overview." In *Canadian Health Care and the State: A Century of Evolution*, edited by C. David Naylor, 125–40. Montreal & Kingston: McGill-Queen's University Press, 1992.

Wengraf, Tom. *Qualitative Research Interviewing*. London: Sage, 2001.
Wittberg, Patricia. "Called to Service: The Changing Institutional Identities of American Denominations." *Nonprofit and Voluntary Sector Quarterly* 29, no. 3 (September 2000): 357–76.
– *From Piety to Professionalism and Back: Transformations of Organized Religious Virtuosity?* Lanham: Lexington Books, 2006.
– *The Rise and Fall of Catholic Religious Orders: A Social Movement Perspective*. New York: The State University of New York Press, 1994.
Yomko, C. "Worshipping the Ground We Walk On: Global Education Associates." http://www.catholicculture.org/culture/library/view.cfm?id=7948.

Contributors

ROSA BRUNO-JOFRÉ (professor and former dean, Faculty of Education, Queen's University; cross-appointed to the Department of History, Faculty of Arts) is a historian and historian of education. She is the author of *Missionary Oblate Sisters: Vision and Mission*, published by McGill-Queen's. Her recent publications include articles in such journals as *Journal of Ecclesiastical History* (Cambridge), *Historical Studies* (Canadian Catholic Association), *Bildungsgeschichte*, *International Journal for the Historiography of Education*, *Paedagogica Historica*, *Hispania Sacra*, *The Catholic Historical Review*, *Educational Theory*, and *Bordón*, among others. She has co-edited with Jon Igelmo Zaldívar *Catholic Education in the Wake of Vatican II* (University of Toronto Press, forthcoming fall 2017). Her research has been funded by the Social Sciences and Humanities Research Council of Canada. She has recently contributed chapters to collections published by Klynhardt, DeBoek, and Routledge. Her work has been translated into French, Spanish, and Chinese. She is senior editor of *Encounters in Theory and History of Education.*

HEIDI MACDONALD (associate professor, University of Lethbridge) is a historian of twentieth-century Canada with specializations in Atlantic Canada, the Great Depression, women religious, and youth. Her recent publications include articles in *Historia de la Educación* and the *Canadian Journal of Sociology*, and chapters in *Bringing Children and Youth into Canadian History: The Difference Kids Make*, edited by Mona Gleason and Tamara Myers (University of British Columbia Press, 2017); *Feminist History in Canada: New Essays on Women, Gender, Work, and Nation*, edited by Catherine Carstairs and Nancy Janovicek (University of British Columbia Press, 2013); and *Vatican II: Expériences Canadiennes – Canadian Experiences*, edited by Michael Attridge, Catherine E. Clifford, and Gilles Routhier (University of Ottawa Press, 2011). Her current Social Sciences and Humanities Research Council–funded project is on women religious in Atlantic Canada since 1960.

ELIZABETH M. SMYTH is professor and vice dean (Programs) at the School of Graduate Studies, University of Toronto. The Social Sciences and Humanities Research Council of Canada has funded her studies of the history of women religious in Canada, the rise of the professions, and the research culture in academic life. She is a senior fellow of Massey College and the University of St Michael's College. Her most recent publications include *Education, Identity and Women Religious: Convents, Classrooms and Colleges*, co-edited with Deirdre Raftery (Routledge, 2016); and *Women Educators, Leaders and Activists: Educational Lives and Networks 1900–1960*, co-edited with Tanya Fitzgerald (Palgrave Macmillan, 2014). For her course of research on the history of women religious, she was awarded the George Edward Clerk Medal for outstanding contribution to Canadian religious history by the Canadian Catholic Historical Association and the Lifetime Achievement Award by the International History of Women Religious Network.

Index